About Island Press

Since 1984, the nonprofit organization Island Press has been stimulating, shaping, and communicating ideas that are essential for solving environmental problems worldwide. With more than 1,000 titles in print and some 30 new releases each year, we are the nation's leading publisher on environmental issues. We identify innovative thinkers and emerging trends in the environmental field. We work with world-renowned experts and authors to develop cross-disciplinary solutions to environmental challenges.

Island Press designs and executes educational campaigns in conjunction with our authors to communicate their critical messages in print, in person, and online using the latest technologies, innovative programs, and the media. Our goal is to reach targeted audiences—scientists, policymakers, environmental advocates, urban planners, the media, and concerned citizens—with information that can be used to create the framework for long-term ecological health and human well-being.

Island Press gratefully acknowledges major support of our work by The Agua Fund, The Andrew W. Mellon Foundation, The Bobolink Foundation, Center for the Living City, The Curtis and Edith Munson Foundation, Forrest C. and Frances H. Lattner Foundation, The JPB Foundation, The Kresge Foundation, The Oram Foundation, Inc., The Overbrook Foundation, The S.D. Bechtel, Jr. Foundation, The Summit Charitable Foundation, Inc., and many other generous supporters.

The opinions expressed in this book are those of the author(s) and do not necessarily reflect the views of our supporters.

design
for
good

design
for
good

**A New Era of Architecture
for Everyone**
John Cary

ISLANDPRESS

Washington | Covelo | London

Island Press is a trademark of The Center for Resource Economics.

Keywords: Affordable housing, architecture, community design process,
design, dignity, green building, health-care design, healthy building,
human-centered design, locally sourced materials, participatory design,
public architecture, public health, public interest design, social equity,
social impact design

This project was made possible in part by the generous support of the
Curry Stone Foundation, the National Endowment for the Arts, and the
Reis Foundation.

Library of Congress Control Number: 2017934969

All Island Press books are printed on environmentally responsible
materials.

Manufactured in the United States of America

10 9 8 7 6 5 4 3 2 1

Designed by Pentagram: Paula Scher, Courtney Gooch

To Courtney Martin, who taught me that buildings
are about people and people are about stories,
and our friend Raymond Lifchez, who has dedicated
his life to the social art of architecture.

Contents

Foreword
Melinda Gates

When I think about the power of design, I think of a visit I once made to a clinic that my friend Paul Farmer runs in Haiti. Paul met me at my car and walked me to the front door, stopping every few steps to greet a patient, offer a hug, ask about someone's family. As we got closer to the building, a lovely garden with a canopy of flowing vines caught my eye. Paul mentioned that he'd planted it himself.

In a country so burdened by poverty and disease, it was striking to think of a physician like Paul making the time to plant a garden. It was a kind gesture, but in the face of so much human suffering, it could also be mistaken for a small one.

Paul, of course, had his reasons. He planted this garden because he wanted his patients and their families to stand in the shade instead of the sun as they waited for care. He planted it because he believed they deserved comfort and the company of something beautiful. He planted it because he wanted more for them in every way possible, and he wanted them to be empowered to expect more for themselves.

When you think about it that way, the garden is no longer just a garden. It's a symbol of empathy, of optimism, of hope. It signals deep compassion and a principled refusal to compromise. That is the power of design.

design for good

As John Cary writes in these pages, design dignifies. It exists not for itself but for those whom it serves. It honors its users—who they are, where they are coming from, what they want to achieve. It proves that their preferences are important and that their voices have been heard. Great design starts with listening, and the product it produces is an expression of empathy.

Before Bill and I started our foundation, I spent a decade working at Microsoft, where I thought about design mostly as it applied to creating new, more user-friendly software. There, I learned that the most important choices we as designers could make were the ones that made our products more accessible to the user. Our research team spent countless hours talking to our customers, learning more about them—their hopes, their frustrations, their comfort with new technologies. The insights they gained helped drive decisions like putting a big button that said "Start" prominently on the screen. For many people, that simple icon managed to transform the personal computer from a source of confusion into one of endless possibility.

Possibility fills the pages of this book as John takes us on a tour of clinics, schools, shelters, and community centers around the world. The spaces we visit are places where bodies will heal, communities will come together, and families will break the cycle of poverty. At each stop, John explains the thoughtful choices that went into creating these sites and gives voice to both the people who designed them and those they were designed for. These structures are intended to be not only landmarks in their communities but also milestones in the lives of the people who will use them.

←
Maternity Waiting Village in Kasungu, Malawi, by MASS Design Group, the University of North Carolina Project–Malawi, and the Malawi Ministry of Health; completed in 2015.

← Women gather and rest at the Maternit Waiting Village in Kasungu, Malawi.

As you turn these pages, let these stories come alive. Imagine what it would be like to be a woman in Malawi traveling from your remote rural home to a Maternity Waiting Village where you will spend the last, most dangerous days of your pregnancy safely within reach of expert medical care. Imagine your anxieties about giving birth someplace so far away and unfamiliar—and your relief at arriving to find it is comfortable, beautiful, and even built with the contours of a pregnant body in mind.

Or imagine what it would be like to have suffered the insecurities of homelessness and the indignities of a life without privacy—but now, finally, to have the simple satisfaction of hearing the door of your own home lock behind you, turned by your own key. Imagine watching a new community meeting space rise from the ground near your home, knowing that the gatherings that will take place there will add new texture to your life, perhaps drawing you into new friendships and beginnings.

The stories in these pages are not merely meant to be read; they are meant to be felt. These photos should not just dazzle you—they should inspire you, uplift you, and even challenge you. They are a reminder that great design is not a finite resource; it is a choice we can all make by listening more, empathizing more, and demanding more for humanity. They call on us all to insist that even in the face of scarcity and suffering, there must always be room for dignity.

The Dignifying Power of Design

One evening as my family was having dinner, my then two-and-a-half-year-old, Maya, froze mid-bite and said, "What's going to happen?" with a frightened look in her eyes.

At first, my wife and I were flummoxed. What was she talking about? We were just sitting there eating our dinner and otherwise enjoying a rare moment of silence.

Except it wasn't silent. We'd been playing the music of Prince constantly since his death. Maya had just heard the dramatic intro to the song "Let's Go Crazy," and it had struck an ominous chord deep inside her.

I've been fascinated to witness how music, not monsters, has the capacity to scare our toddler. It organizes her experience on some deep subconscious level—triggering her fight-or-flight response or filling her with a joyful impulse to dance.

I believe that this is how design functions in our lives—like the soundtrack that we're not even fully aware is playing. It sends us subconscious messages about how to feel and what to expect. Just as my daughter, who has an entirely untrained ear, can hear a few chords and sense that something is off, I think each of us has an organic way of processing the signals that design sends us.

It's what environmental psychologists have described as "place identity"—essentially that the foremost building blocks of our sense of self are actually the spaces in which we live, work, and play. It's what I have come to simply call dignity.

Dignity is to design what justice is to law and health is to medicine. In the simplest of terms, for me, dignity is about knowing your intrinsic worth and seeing that worth reflected in the places you inhabit. It's about being primed for your full potential.

Dignity is a kid in rural China learning in a colorful classroom that makes him feel valued and piques his curiosity. Dignity is a public space in Atlanta where young and old, rich and poor alike mingle, celebrate, and play. Dignity is a cancer patient in a light-filled hospital ward in rural Rwanda with lots of natural airflow to support her healing.

Almost nothing influences the quality of our lives more than the design of our homes, our schools, our workplaces, and our public spaces. Yet design is taken for granted. People don't realize they deserve better or that better is even possible. Like my daughter, they are affected by design but don't know how to name what is happening. This book aims to change that.

The following pages capture character-driven, real-world stories from across the globe about design that dignifies. I hope these stories will awaken a new and unexpected understanding of the ways that design shapes our lives. I hope this book gives the average person the tools necessary to seek out and demand dignifying design. Likewise, I hope it gives designers the opportunity to reconnect with what drew them to the work in the first place and, perhaps, some practical ideas about how to put dignity at the center of their practice.

This isn't just another book for and about designers. It's a book about the lives we lead, inextricably shaped by the spaces and places we inhabit. For too long, design has been seen as a luxury, the province of the rich, not the poor, who often need it most. That can no longer be acceptable to those of us in the design field, nor to those affected by the field's too often anemic moral imagination, which is to say, absolutely everybody.

The central premise of the book is this: *everyone deserves good design.*

↖
Sharon Fields in Clifton Forge, Virginia, by design/buildLAB; completed in 2015.

Decoding Design

If you asked one hundred random people or even one hundred designers "What is design?" you would get approximately that many different answers. In the most positive sense, this explains the pervasiveness of designers working in and touching every imaginable aspect of our lives. Beyond built structures, such as the ones that fill this book, the products we rely on day in and day out, the services we use as members of society, are all designed.

We designers have long stumbled over how to capture this reality—that design is so pervasive and people have so many perceptions of it, if it is even in their consciousness. This has especially been the case for those of us who are trying to expand design's reach beyond its traditional, elite client base. In the past few decades we've struggled with nomenclature: what to call this growing field of practice that focuses on engaging entirely new communities and populations?

For years, in my role as executive director of the nonprofit Public Architecture, I advocated for and advanced the term "public interest design," akin to the well-developed fields of public interest law and public health. These fields serve the public en masse and at a level that the traditional practices of law and medicine still rarely manage to achieve. To my mind, if designers modeled their engagement after what was already working in other professions, it had a shot at reaching scale, further and faster.

In framing public interest design, I tried to cast a wide net, identifying buildings, products, and services created for and with disenfranchised communities. In some ways, the term was a great accelerator for the movement. People recognized the parallel in other fields, and it legitimized the practice quickly. In other ways, it allowed this kind of work to remain marginalized, just as it does in law and medicine. Rather than helping it to be seen as an approach that should transform all design, the qualifier distinguished it, for better or worse.

An equal number of designers—especially in the product and service spaces—have utilized the term "social impact design." Such work directly favors community, environmental, or humanitarian causes and the change it can create. Of the array used to describe design for the public good, this term is perhaps the most closely aligned with social justice.

The term that has actually gained the greatest traction in recent years is "human-centered design," popularized by the innovation guru IDEO and its nonprofit spinoff, IDEO.org. These two interrelated entities have done much more than simply brand a term. Instead, they have built an ecosystem of resources—a field guide, an interactive website, an online course, and a body of work—to teach and demonstrate its application. It raises an important question, however: What is design if not human centered? Who or what is it designed for?

Those of us who care deeply about this work have been treading water in a sea of terms for too long. Language matters. Without having a shared, clear vocabulary to unify around, the field has often felt disjointed, at best, and competitive, at worst. Recent graduates don't always know how to find the kinds of opportunities they crave. Designers looking for philanthropic funding aren't taken seriously. And most important of all, those who need design most—regular people—aren't even sure how to describe what it is they desire in their environments, products, and services.

In the dozens of interviews that I conducted for this book—speaking with beneficiaries, creators, and funders of design from around the world—there was one term or word used universally: "design." The qualifiers that were once useful may have finally outlived their usefulness. I now see those qualifiers themselves doing exactly the opposite of their intent, which is to recognize design at its purest and best.

Defining Dignity

Another term, "dignity," warrants a closer look. I use the term here quite specifically and true to its definition: "the state or quality of being worthy of honor or respect." I can't remember exactly when I first coupled it with "design," but I know that ever since, it's felt exactly right. For the purpose of confirming my hunch about that instinct, I went back and looked at the origins of the word.

It turns out that "dignity" was first used popularly in the seventeenth and eighteenth centuries in precisely the opposite way I use it here—to confer status. Only royalty had dignity; it was not yet seen as universal or intrinsic.

But that connotation shifted over time, kick-started by the German philosopher Immanuel Kant, who wrote that dignity was "an unconditional, incomparable value" in his 1785 book *Groundwork of the Metaphysics of Morals*. I'm no philosopher, and much of Kant's writing flies above my head, but central to his thesis is the idea that dignity is inextricably linked with self-determination. In his way of thinking, we can defy the rules of nature and set our own course, and this is what distinguishes us from other species. This, in other words, is what makes us human and universally worthy of dignity.

The moral framework for modern human rights grew from this seed. Dignity found its way into the 1945 United Nations Charter—"We the peoples of the United Nations . . . reaffirm faith in fundamental human rights, in the dignity and worth of the human person." It is also in the 1948 Universal Declaration of Human Rights, which states that "recognition of the inherent dignity and of the equal and inalienable rights of all members of the human family is the foundation of freedom, justice, and peace in the world." Today, almost every constitution in the world includes the word "dignity."

Michael Rosen, professor of government at Harvard University and author of the 2012 book *Dignity: Its History and Meaning*, reminds us, however, that the sources of this powerful word are not just academic but also spiritual: "'Dignity' appears frequently in faith-based ethical discourse. Although not the rhetorical property of any single religion, it is most prominent in Catholic thought."

I have to admit, I was a little bewildered to discover that the religion of my childhood, the one I have mostly rejected, has crept back into my life in the form of this now favorite word of mine. But the truth is that I grew disenchanted with Catholicism not because of the ideas but because of the hypocrisy I witnessed within the church. Yet the doctrine of dignity—the notion that all people deserve to have their basic needs met, without judgment or exception—has always resonated with me on a deep level.

In the Jesuit tradition, I frequently did "service work" in my hometown, Milwaukee, Wisconsin. For an entire year of my youth, I spent almost every weekend swinging a hammer, hanging drywall, and painting at a Habitat for Humanity site on Cherry Street—in a mostly poor, almost entirely black community near my Jesuit college preparatory high school. I got to know the single mother and her three small children who would come to own the house as we worked side by side. It was meaningful, physical work.

Dorothy Day, social activist and Catholic convert, articulates why this means so much to me as no architect ever has:

"What we would like to do is change the world—make it a little simpler for people to feed, clothe, and shelter themselves as God intended them to do. And, by fighting for better conditions, by crying out unceasingly for the rights of the workers, the poor, of the destitute—the rights of the worthy and the unworthy poor, in other words—we can, to a certain extent, change the world; we can work for the oasis, the little cell of joy and peace in a harried world."

What more powerful goal could a person have than to collaborate in the design of that "little cell of joy and peace in a harried world," as Day wrote? She understood, as too few designers have, that shelter is not a matter of simply having a roof over one's head. It is the ultimate symbol of uncompromising worthiness.

And yet, I look back on that formative experience with some inner conflict. I realize that I did contribute to restoring that family's sense of dignity. That was a good, even a great, thing. But I ultimately got back into my parents' tan minivan and drove home to the suburbs without a systemic critique of the dynamics that I was a part of as one of the tools in my proverbial tool belt. Design that dignifies, if it's to be truly radical at the root, can't just comfort but must also render poorly designed spaces as unacceptable. It must engage not just one plot of land at a time but the system that continues to create indignity in the first place.

The need for systemic reform, not just redignifying one-offs, is at the heart of much of the work of Jacqueline Novogratz, founder of the nonprofit Acumen. I've been inspired by her take on dignity:

"Dignity for me is being able to have choice and opportunity. . . . [People must] deal with each other as equals. It is in that interaction that you see a sense of human dignity, that they have something to offer each other, that they have an ability to transform each other, but it comes from starting with this assumption that we can extend that value that all of us are created equal to every human being on the planet. That each of us is capable."

If I overlay this wisdom on design, here is what I know in my bones: Once you see what design can do, you can't unsee it. And once you experience dignity, you can't accept anything less. Both become a part of your "possible."

design for good

Beyond Good Intentions

The power of design to dignify will never be fully explored until average people have some sense that they deserve better. Which is why I'm so committed to speaking with nondesigners and designers alike.

Although I was trained as an architect, my career has focused more on communication than on design or construction in any traditional sense. I've written for major news outlets, initially struggling to describe design in clear and accessible language rather than in the jargon so many design professionals subscribe to. Through my work with thought leadership entities such as TED and the Aspen Institute, I've also had the chance to bring a diverse array of designers to some of the world's biggest stages to tell their stories and humanize the practice.

Still, a lack of awareness persists about how this socially oriented practice of design has evolved and matured. While there has been a steady uptick in media coverage—led in no small part by the *New York Times*' architecture critic, Michael Kimmelman, who has made design for the public good central to his writing—the vast majority of press focuses almost solely on designers' intentions. Rarely are the voices of clients and actual users presented. Clients are sometimes offered a token quote or mention in the project credits but often nothing more. The result is that we're hearing barely half of the story and limiting our ability to fully understand the impact of design.

↑
Ánimo Leadership Charter
High School in Inglewood,
California, by Brooks +
Scarpa and Green Dot Public
Schools; completed in 2012.

The Dignifying Power of Design

At every level, design is a matrix of relationships—from clients who make decisions about projects to designers who bring life to those clients' visions. In between, in a health-care setting, for example, are users who range from doctors and nurses to patients and family visitors, among many others. Then, especially in the case of building projects, there are those who give physical form to the structures: construction workers, artisans, craftspeople, and scores of others.

In recent years, design for the public good has also matured and changed substantially—from conceptual shipping container health clinics to landmark facilities such as the Butaro Hospital in rural Rwanda, the subject of chapter 1. Accordingly, this book focuses on built projects completed in the past five years.

From Atlanta to Angdong, Dallas to Dhaka, some of the best of this new body of work is not just beautifully designed and constructed but also painstakingly documented by world-class photographers and filmmakers once reserved for only the most elite of projects. This imagery and storytelling has been essential in elevating design for the public good to its rightful place alongside other forms of design, again without the need for special categories or commendations.

This is especially the case for one entity, whose work accounts for a disproportionate number of projects in this book. MASS Design Group, a nonprofit with offices in Boston and Kigali as well as work around the world, has put design on the map in a way few others have. I have had a front seat view of the organization's work and growth since its inception, covering it through my writing, quietly marshaling philanthropic funds to support it, and advising and encouraging its leadership as they chart a bold new path for design.

In the chapters that follow, deep dives into the work of MASS bookend a collection of projects by other entities around the world. Every project in the book is presented equally through the eyes and words of clients and users, when those two groups differ, as well as the designers. Their insights and stories are accompanied by colorful and vibrant photographs, along with facts and figures about each project. I've aimed to take this book far beyond designers' good intentions to capture the impact of design on those clients, those users, and all of us.

Design Dignifies

My wife, Courtney Martin, an award-winning journalist who often writes about social justice issues, claims to have known nothing about design before we met a handful of years ago. Like many people, she thought design was little more than a luxury for the rich. She assumed it had almost nothing to do with her and certainly had very little to do with the activists and social entrepreneurs she was writing about on a regular basis.

But as I showed her comfortable waiting rooms in health clinics, and community centers that looked like children's museums—tactile, playful, and bright—she realized that everyone deserves good design. She came to understand that design is, in fact, a foundational building block of the kind of social justice she was so hell-bent on writing about and fighting for.

The words of one of her literary heroes, Virginia Woolf, took on new meaning. It wasn't just "a room of one's own" that women and other historically disenfranchised people needed; it was "a well-designed room of one's own." Beauty, she realized, is not a luxury.

For my part, I have always been a deep believer in design, but before I met Courtney, my career largely involved speaking to and for designers themselves. I realized that I had been advocating on behalf of the public without truly engaging them, hearing them. My first book, *The Power of Pro Bono: 40 Stories about Design for the Public Good by Architects and Their Clients*, became the first design book ever to present the client's voice equally with that of the designer. Seven years on, this book very well may be only the second to do so. Rather than the interview transcriptions that constituted my first book, the interviews for this book are presented as reported narratives and contextualized whenever possible.

As with Courtney, I want this book to awaken in people from all walks of life the realization that they too deserve good design. I believe this book can be a clarion call for all of us—designers and nondesigners alike—to demand more, not just from one another but for and with one another.

I want this to be the book that challenges conventional wisdom and shatters misperceptions about design—that it costs more and is only a luxury. It is so much more powerful, particularly when applied to some of our world's most intractable challenges. Design can be life-affirming and life-changing; in short, design dignifies.

1.

If It Can Happen Here

The Improbable Story of Rwanda's Butaro Hospital

→
Butaro Hospital in Burera, Rwanda, by MASS Design Group, Partners in Health, and Rwanda Ministry of Health; completed in 2011.

Michael Murphy remembers the night well. On the eve of his final semester presentation during his first year at the Harvard Graduate School of Design, Murphy quietly ventured across campus to sit in on a lecture unrelated to his pressing schoolwork. It was December 1, 2006, World AIDS Day.

The lecturer was the global health pioneer Dr. Paul Farmer, cofounder of Partners in Health (PIH), an international nongovernmental organization. A year earlier, while living in South Africa, Murphy had read *Mountains Beyond Mountains*, Tracy Kidder's popular book on Farmer, an uncompromising humanitarian, and the organization he cofounded. Before ultimately deciding to go to architecture school, Murphy had even researched job openings at PIH. Then and now, he faced the dilemma many of us have—how do you get access to an organization that you admire? A friend who wasn't even in graduate school with Murphy had alerted him to Farmer's lecture, so off he went.

Murphy was preparing to pull an "all-nighter," a rite of passage in architecture school, to work on his final project. He had done so innumerable times that semester, and each time, he had a little ritual of wearing his father's old Poughkeepsie High School Crew sweatshirt. Murphy recalls: "I looked terrible, ragged, unkempt, wearing this paint-covered sweatshirt."

Soon after Murphy settled into his seat, Farmer said, "We're building housing." Murphy had never thought about housing as a health-care priority before. "That really piqued my interest, and I sat up, thinking, 'Wow, this guy is building housing for people in really poor communities because he wants to provide better health care.' It instantly made sense: housing is a social determinant of health."

← View of the countryside surrounding the Butaro Hospital.

Farmer has a practice of patiently hearing out every person in line to talk with him after a lecture or panel discussion. "He's very, very kind," Murphy tells me, "and I think he was really energized that night by all the students who came up to him afterward, saying 'I want to mention my project to you.' He just waits for everyone to finish. That access was surprising; he was just so receptive."

Eager to work for any architecture firm working with Farmer, Murphy asked which firms Partners in Health had experience with. After all, Farmer had described building clinics, hospitals, housing, even roads. "I drew the last clinic on a napkin," Farmer told him. Here was a pioneer in global health who was undertaking significant building projects, and he had effectively never worked with an architect. Murphy was astonished, unaware at the time how little the practices of architecture and design intersected with global health and development work such as Farmer's.

At the end of their conversation, Farmer gave Murphy his e-mail address. By 9:30 p.m., Murphy was back at his desk and writing an e-mail to Farmer rather than working on his final project. "I sent him a message, and he wrote right back to me. So I sent him another e-mail, and he wrote right back again," Murphy recalls. "We were e-mailing about gardens and fishponds at his hospital in Haiti, and just talking about the beauty of gardens. I couldn't believe that this guy was writing back to me." Murphy remembers feeling a little starstruck but also inspired by the access to Farmer.

Murphy finally turned back to his studio project. He was tasked with squeezing a public pool into a bizarre, awkward site near a train station in Brookline, Massachusetts. "It was meaningless. I was also totally failing on the project," he recalls. But Murphy finished the project, and kept in touch with Farmer. In the summer of 2007, just six months after meeting him, Murphy accepted Farmer's invitation to visit Rwanda, one of the countries in which PIH had recently started to work.

Twenty-seven at the time, Murphy had never been to Rwanda, a land-locked East African country known for its gorillas and volcanoes and for the brutal civil war that had led to a horrendous genocide in 1994, just over a decade earlier. In its healing and under the leadership of President Paul Kagame since 2000, Rwanda had been transforming itself into a center for innovation in health-care delivery. PIH signed on as a crucial partner of Rwanda's Ministry of Health in 2005.

Mere hours after Murphy arrived in the capital city, Kigali, a doctor named Michael Rich picked him up for the two-hour drive to the organization's main office in Rwinkwavu, a town in eastern Rwanda. As he drove, Rich effectively said to Murphy, "What are you doing here? You're clearly not here for long enough to make a difference."

Murphy would learn during their drive that Rich's father was a contractor who had done huge building projects. Rich himself had built his own house out of mud bricks. So Rich uniquely understood construction and building and had done a lot of thinking about the planning of PIH's medical campus in Rwinkwavu.

Speaking of Rich, Murphy tells me, "Michael is very talented in a design sense. He was understandably asking, 'What's this twenty-seven-year-old architecture student with barely one year of experience doing here for a few weeks? What value is that going to provide?'" Murphy concedes, "He was very skeptical. I would have the same feeling if I was bringing on someone like that today."

Over many months and years, the two developed a strong relationship built on trust, hard work, and mutual commitment to PIH's goals. Murphy now counts Rich as one of his dearest friends and biggest advocates. "It was in that first couple of weeks, living with a bunch of doctors, trying to make myself useful, that I really built these relationships," Murphy explains. "It also helped me at least start to hone in on what would be useful for me to do."

Murphy's time in Rwanda that summer was spent between Kigali and Rwinkwavu, with visits to other PIH field sites. The organization had an array of projects and facilities, and Murphy tried to help out wherever possible. Perhaps most significantly, it was then that he met a Rwandan builder named Bruce Nizeye, PIH's head of infrastructure at the time. Nizeye was doing everything from building a large training center and a laundry facility to putting in a garden and a fishpond in one of the other health centers. Murphy recalls innumerable small projects that Nizeye, his brother Fabrice Nusenga, and an army of local artisans tackled day in and day out. They were working out of a few old warehouses on the PIH campus, left over from a mining company that used to be there.

"I was just so inspired. Bruce and his crew were thinking about architecture completely differently from how I ever had. He was literally making everything—working with carpenters to make furniture and metalworkers to weld windows, among many other things," Murphy recalls. "But being so young and so new to architecture, I wasn't burdened by the way architecture is made in the U.S. enough to understand exactly how different it really was. There, if someone needed a chair, Bruce made a chair."

Nizeye's focus on local labor and local materials made a profound impression on Murphy, and it would become a hallmark of Murphy's work and the nonprofit he would go on to found. Murphy stuck close to Nizeye, working on the laundry facility and other small projects, before returning to the United States and to school.

I met Michael Murphy shortly after his return from that first fateful trip to Rwanda, for no other reason than that he was dating a summer intern at the nonprofit I directed in San Francisco. I had heard a lot about Murphy by the time the pair waltzed into the fourth-floor loft that our organization occupied.

When Murphy and my intern, a Bay Area native named Marika Shioiri-Clark, told me they were returning to Rwanda to design and build a hospital, my first thought was, "This is a terrible idea." In my work domestically and knowing of innumerable other examples internationally, I had seen well-intentioned designers parachuting into unfamiliar places to "help," only to be crushed by the complexity of conditions they never could have anticipated from a distance. This seemed all the more probable for a couple of Ivy League graduate students. What could they possibly have been thinking?

At the time, most work of this type was conceptual, and much of it was small in scale, if it had even reached the point of construction. Schemes for shipping-container clinics were especially prevalent. Again, all well-intentioned but difficult to execute for a whole host of reasons.

Thank goodness Murphy and Shioiri-Clark didn't listen to me.

The pair and a group of classmates launched MASS Design Group, with MASS standing for "Model of Architecture Serving Society." Along with classmate David Saladik, Murphy and Shioiri-Clark went to Rwanda that winter. They spent their school break sketching possible schemes for a hospital in the Burera District, which at the time was home to over 340,000 people and barely one functioning clinic. They then returned to Harvard, recruited a larger group of students, and spent many cold Boston nights and weekends designing the hospital.

After weeks of work, the team settled on a barrack-style building for the hospital. Even Murphy was underwhelmed. "It was not a good design; we just didn't know what we were doing," he recalls. Murphy shared the design with Michael Rich, who told him, "I really don't think this is what you want to show. It's not the kind of inspiring architecture that we were hoping for." Murphy knew Rich was right. He and his classmates were designing far from Rwanda; they needed to be back there, living on-site, working side by side with PIH and the community.

Murphy and Saladik moved to Rwanda in the summer of 2008, living on what is now the Butaro Hospital site. The hilltop where the hospital stands was itself a contested site and a prison during Rwanda's civil war in 1994; PIH had converted an old jail building into its quarters. Murphy and Saladik shared bunks with PIH staff and immersed themselves in the community and the site.

"We were drawing all day in our room or elsewhere and, at night, showing plans and interviewing nurses and doctors," Murphy recalls. "We presented the various layouts and went back and forth with them. It was this very, very intimate, iterative design process, happening with medical professionals on a day-to-day basis. It was so ideal." More than designing the building together, Murphy, Saladik, and PIH were building relationships rooted in trust and understanding.

Because of its connections with Brigham and Women's Hospital in Boston and other major medical systems, PIH was able to attract some of the world's best-trained doctors to Rwanda. "They knew how an operating theater at the Brigham should be configured," Murphy recalls, "but no one knew how it should be configured in this remote context, which didn't even have reliable electricity at the time. There was an expectation that it had to be different. Because of that, I think, people were willing to go along with us on this journey."

↑
**Visitors congregate outside
a Butaro Hospital ward.**

design for good

A young physician within PIH, Dr. Peter Drobac, would come to play an important role in this project. A native of my hometown, Milwaukee, Drobac had led a parallel life to Murphy's in some important ways. Drobac took his first trip outside the United States at age twenty-one, when he visited the African country of Tanzania to study primate ecology and behavior. While the primate study didn't convince Drobac of a future in that particular field, he fell in love with the people and culture of Tanzania and returned the following year.

The year was 1998, and the HIV epidemic was raging in sub-Saharan Africa. It was just a couple of years after the first effective HIV treatments became widely available in developed countries. "I found myself sitting right at the nexus of this vast gulf of inequality, where most of the kids we were seeing and working with were coming in from villages where they had lost family members to HIV," Drobac recalls. "We were surrounded by communities that were dying." He had read and knew about effective treatments that weren't reaching the immense suffering in Tanzania, and it filled him with anger.

When he returned to the United States to attend medical school, Drobac knew that he wanted to do something about these vast disparities in health and wealth around the world. He was particularly committed to returning to East Africa. But he had no inkling of how to go about it. Global health wasn't such a clearly defined field at that time.

"I went to the Medical College of Wisconsin, and I recall meeting an administrator the first week and telling him what I wanted to do," Drobac says. "The counsel I got was, basically, 'Okay, that's nice. You can do some missions when you finish your residency. But, for right now, just focus on your education.' There were no resources, there were no mentors, there was nothing happening."

In medical school, Drobac was somehow turned on to the writing of PIH founder Dr. Paul Farmer. In Farmer, Drobac found someone who seemed just as angry as he was. "But he had a framework for understanding what was happening and what these dynamics were," Drobac concedes. Shortly thereafter, Drobac moved to Boston, where Partners in Health is based, for a residency at three local hospitals through Harvard University. Work with PIH soon took Drobac to Rwanda.

By 2005, PIH was officially engaged in Rwanda, working with the Clinton Foundation's HIV/AIDS initiative in the southeastern part of the country. The goal was to treat people living with HIV in a place where the disease was rampant and, in so doing, build a bona fide health-care system.

Just a year later, President Bill Clinton was in Rwinkwavu visiting with Farmer and government officials. After seeing PIH's approach firsthand, Clinton declared, "I think this is the model that can save Africa."

That may have been hyperbole, but the endorsement was galvanizing. The entire country of Rwanda would go on to adopt PIH's model of community-based primary health care. It decentralized health services in each of the country's thirty districts, with a designated hospital in each district. Those hospitals would be supplemented by a network of outpatient health centers farther afield, which fed into a network of community health workers who managed to reach patients in even more rural settings. It was called the District Health Systems Strengthening framework.

The first test case was the Burera District, starting in late 2007. "Our notion was, let's go to the worst-off district in the country—the place with the poorest health outcomes and the weakest infrastructure—and make it a proof of concept," Drobac explains. Farmer's theory was "If it can happen here, it can happen anywhere."

At that time, this district of more than 340,000 people had no hospital and only one doctor. There was a small patchwork network of health services, usually with about two nurses, very poor facilities, and often no electricity. Burera was, however, a region that President Kagame had campaigned in, promising to build a hospital. Even with the hospital mandate, PIH and the Ministry of Health didn't set out to build a flagship hospital. They simply set out to build an integrated health-care system with a hospital at its core.

Although Drobac had been stationed in Rwanda since 2005, it wasn't until January 2008 that he went to the Burera District to concentrate his work. It was there that he met Murphy, Shioiri-Clark, and Saladik during another one of their extended visits. Drobac recalls noticing that they were a little younger than he was. "I liked Michael, Marika, and David instantly."

↖
US president Bill Clinton,
joined by daughter Chelsea
Clinton, Dr. Paul Farmer,
and Rwandan leaders, at the
hospital's groundbreaking
ceremony.

↑
People gather on a hillside
to see President Clinton
speak.

→
Local laborers, many of
them women who were not
previously present on
construction sites, prepare
the hospital site.

On August 6, 2008, two years after drawing attention to the potential of Rwanda's health system, Bill Clinton spoke at the ceremonial ground-breaking for the Butaro Hospital. "I believe this hospital, sitting in this beautiful, peaceful setting, symbolizes health and hope and peace and unity," he said. "Everything about this hospital, including this beautiful setting, symbolizes the future that I believe we all want for Rwanda, for all of Africa, and for all of the world. It is about everything that is good about our future and overcoming the parts of the past that have to be dealt with."

A few months later, as their families back home were celebrating Thanksgiving, Murphy and the team stood on that lush hilltop as the hospital officially broke ground. In the intervening months, an excavator had proved too costly to bring to the site, a four-hour, dirt road drive from Kigali, so on that day local community members started digging the huge foundation themselves, with shovels.

From that day forward, dozens and often hundreds of people were working on the job site. Under Nizeye's direction, nearly four thousand local people were hired and trained to help build the hospital. Many were entirely new to construction, learning invaluable skills. Construction crews were organized into six teams, each working a two-week shift, enabling six times as many people to be hired. The workers not only were paid for their time but also received food, water, and health care. These efforts didn't cost more; they actually saved money. All told, MASS and PIH were able to reduce the hospital's cost to roughly two-thirds that of comparable hospitals in Rwanda.

Because of the cost and time required to transport an excavator from Rwanda's capital city, Kigali, the Butaro Hospital site was excavated by local laborers.

A mason works on the lava rock walls of the Butaro Doctors' Housing.

The workers had to be flexible. Murphy, Saladik, and their team were still designing as construction got under way. "At one point, I turned to Dave and said, 'This building is not going to be a great piece of architecture; there are too many constraints. We have the capability to do only two or maybe three things,'" Murphy recalls. "'Let's just focus on those three simple things, and then the next building we do together, that might be great.'"

The three physical elements that the design team prioritized were a local materials palette, a sloped shed roof to aid airflow, and wards with the beds configured to face windows. Situated on a hilltop with a very dynamic topography, the project deliberately broke from any standard hospital design, looking overall more like a college campus.

First, in addition to typical materials such as stucco and tile, volcanic lava rock was used for the exterior walls. The masons experimented with tightly set cut rocks rather than the thick mortar walls often associated with lava rock in the region. The technique revealed the beauty of the stone, affording a nearly seamless expanse of deep gray porous walls, which would become one of the hospital's most defining aesthetic characteristics.

The masons—many of them women—honed their craft as they worked. In fact, when they later returned to the first lava rock wall they had completed, they insisted on tearing it down and redoing it to match the excellence of the newer sections. The masons had become passionate about their innovation. They are now sought after in other parts of the community and region for their one-of-a-kind crafts(wo)manship.

One of the lead masons on the hospital was Anne-Marie Nyiranshimi-yimana, who said of the experience, "I will stay a mason. It got stuck in me. What made me continue to like it is it dignified me. Where I stand now, I am happy. Everything is because of the hospital project. No amount of value can be assigned to dignity. We really can't count the true value of dignity."

Although there were very few female masons at the time, there was one on a popular BBC radio program in Rwanda. The character's name was Kankwanzi, a nickname soon attached to Nyiranshimiyimana. "There are now many women," she says, "all of them building. That's what we do, really—we do miracles. They are miracles if you really pay attention."

Attention was needed in other areas as well. The MASS team learned that the design of some clinics and hospitals in Rwanda actually caused many patients to get sicker because infected air became trapped in the small, poorly ventilated rooms. In consultation with PIH, infectious disease experts such as Edward Nardell from the Harvard T.H. Chan School of Public Health, and researchers from the Centers for Disease Control and Prevention, MASS made a series of innovative design decisions to change that. Together, their efforts represent the second major design move. The hospital's pitched roofs mimic shed roofs seen all over Rwanda, creating an organic feel, but they also enable inclusion

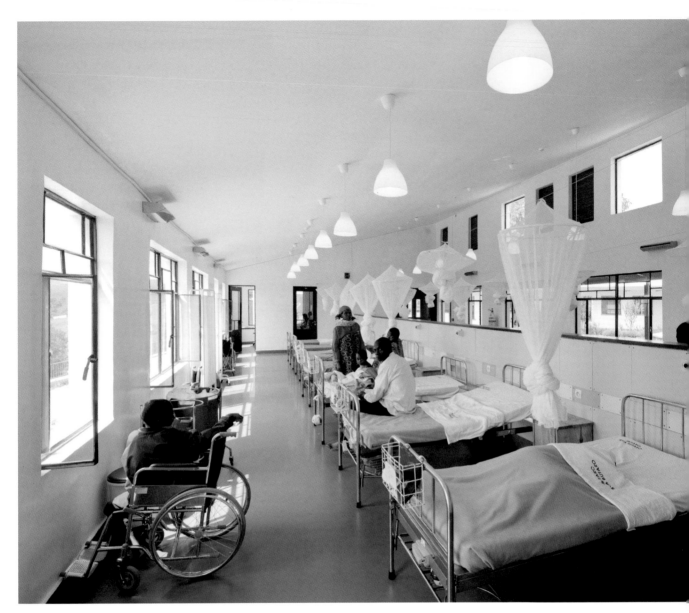

↑
Patients and family
members rest in a
recovery ward at the
Butaro Hospital.

design for good

of a clerestory—an extra row of windows below the higher side of the roof—which creates more airflow and provides crucial ventilation.

MASS also eliminated interior corridors entirely, including waiting rooms, where transmission of diseases can be especially high, and installed very large radius ceiling fans donated by a company called Big Ass Solutions. The low-speed fans with diameters of up to twenty-four feet keep air flowing through the wards and out louvered windows. Germicidal ultraviolet lights, designed to kill or inactivate microbes, and durable, easy-to-clean flooring with a nonpermeable, continuous surface—free of joints and grooves where harmful bacteria could take root—also contributed to the healthier design.

The third major design move was to make the wards centrally loaded. That basically means that the key support systems, such as wiring for electricity, run through the middle of the wards on a half-wall approximately five feet tall. And, again, rather than using a traditional hospital room configuration—where beds are placed next to windows, if the rooms are afforded natural light at all—each bed directly faces a window. Patients look into the calm courtyard of the hospital or out over the breathtaking hillside and valleys surrounding the hospital.

"It's funny, in retrospect, when I look back, the extreme constraints are really what make it a successful design," Murphy acknowledges. "That's actually what people point to as success: the architecture, its simplicity, and its simple moves. Those things totally changed the way I understand how to evaluate architecture. I thought it was a total compromise and a failure, but it actually turned out to be our path to success."

When I asked Murphy what it was like to see the hospital rise from the earth, he reminded me that he returned to finish graduate school while colleagues Sierra Bainbridge and Garret Gantner led the on-site construction from MASS's standpoint. "When I returned to see the hospital nearly complete, it was one of the most powerful experiences of my life," Murphy explains. "It was just completely mind-blowing to see something constructed from what you drew, albeit with significant adjustments as construction progressed."

The Butaro Hospital opened in 2011, serving 21,000 people in its first year. Beyond the thousands involved in its construction, the hospital employed 270, most of them locals, in an area with chronic unemployment. Its patient base and staff have only expanded since that time.

Before long, the Butaro Hospital became a sought-after destination for PIH donors and global health advocates interested in learning about its community-engaging, disease-preventing design. The tour guide, often Drobac, would always shuffle by the former jail building, still the main living quarters for visiting doctors, often with an apology. Everyone recognized that the recruitment and retention of doctors were paramount and that both depended on better conditions.

This is how MASS and PIH's next collaborative project on the Butaro site—four duplex houses for eight on-site and visiting doctors—was born. With Nizeye having moved on from PIH toward the end of the hospital construction to start his own company, MASS took the lead role in not just designing but also building the doctors' housing, directing the workforce of local laborers.

Sited along the steep hillside, the structures were built with compressed stabilized earth blocks—a brick produced with soil excavated from the site. The project created 900 jobs for community members, who were trained in sustainable building practices. The houses opened a year later, in 2012.

I had a chance to visit the Butaro Hospital and the new housing shortly thereafter, and I marveled at the spatial experience, the quality of construction—complete with the signature lava rock walls—and the handmade furniture. Quite literally, my only concern was that doctors might not want to leave after living in the units. The buildings are that beautiful, as is the surrounding scenery.

Meanwhile, as Rwanda's new country director for PIH, succeeding Michael Rich, Drobac was working with the government on a major expansion of health-care services across the Burera District. PIH had trained 1,500 health-care workers in every village in the district and had helped to rehabilitate, build, or support seventeen health centers in the district—all feeding into the Butaro Hospital.

With all this momentum, Drobac and PIH saw potential for the Burera District to become something of an innovation hub for the rest of the country. Around that time, Drobac was summoned to meet with the minister of health, who thanked PIH for its assistance and leadership with diseases such as HIV, tuberculosis, and malaria. The minister wanted to refocus the organization's efforts on the growing challenges facing the country via noncommunicable diseases—cancer, diabetes, and heart disease, to name a few.

"As soon as the Butaro Hospital opened, we suddenly had an ambitious new project for which this big, new hospital was actually not really designed or equipped," Drobac explains. PIH made the decision to retrofit one of the wards into an inpatient cancer ward. It also expanded one of the laboratories into what is now one of the top pathology labs on the continent.

With the majority of cancer care services, including chemotherapy, delivered on an outpatient basis, PIH decided to build a separate facility adjacent to the hospital. Drobac explains that even at the well-known

Dana-Farber Cancer Institute in Boston, there are only a couple of
floors where people go on an inpatient basis. Most cancer patients are
never, or only rarely, admitted to the hospital; they come in for the day
and get their treatment.

The Butaro Cancer Center of Excellence, as it is called, opened in 2013
and is the first comprehensive cancer center in East Africa. MASS
designed it on the foundation of an existing building. A wall of large,
operable glass doors afford expansive views of hillsides and the Virunga
mountain range beyond. Here again, MASS and PIH prioritized skills
training in the facility's construction, employing over 550 people.

As with the Butaro Hospital just up the hill, ventilation was a major
consideration in the design of the cancer center. Laborers installed
similar large fans to aid airflow, along with germicidal ultraviolet lights,
again to neutralize harmful pathogens. Most important, the cancer
center, like the hospital, keeps all circulation and waiting areas on the
exterior of the building to avoid exposing patients with weakened
immune systems to infection.

The latest addition to the Butaro campus is a cluster of shared housing
for the hospital staff. The three units form a communal-style compound
for up to fifteen medical professionals. The buildings are more angular
in form than previous projects, but they were constructed with the
same commitment to local labor and materials.

design for good

If It Can Happen Here

→
Colorful interior of a treatment area in the Butaro Cancer Center of Excellence, with large fans for air circulation.

↓
Butaro Cancer Center of Excellence, juxtaposed with a brick building that predated it on the site.

Today, Drobac and PIH are deep into yet another history-making initiative: creating the first University of Global Health Equity, within sight of the Butaro campus. "Partners in Health has always been a learning organization and engaged in lots of educational and training programs," Drobac explains. "But this is a whole new institution dedicated to advancing this field and reimagining how we train health professionals and future health-care leaders."

Drobac goes on: "Rwanda has been such a hotbed of innovation in health-care delivery and a remarkable example of delivering high-quality health care with great outcomes. At a population level, we're doing this with very little money and with a preferential treatment for the poor. We felt like it would be incredible to try to distill some of these lessons, which we feel are transferable to the rest of the world."

In 2015, the university welcomed its first class of master's candidates in global health delivery, totaling 52 as of this writing. The campus will be built in phases and is being sited on two hilltops near the Butaro campus, with a land area totaling roughly 250 acres. When the new campus opens, in the fall of 2018, PIH plans to have a medical school, followed by nursing and midwifery programs. PIH intends to expand each program and add new programs roughly every year, reaching approximately 1,000 full-time students from the African continent and around the world a decade from now.

Ground was broken on the first phase of the new campus in late 2016. The Boston-based architecture and planning firm Shepley Bulfinch led the master planning for the campus, while MASS took responsibility for the student housing and landscape.

"As someone who has been in the Burera District since early 2008, when the infrastructure was so poor and there was just a lot of unnecessary suffering, it's been immensely gratifying to watch the transformation of the community," Drobac says proudly. "It's not just about the hospital but also about the development of the town and the communities around the hospital; so many folks who we worked with and laid bricks with on the hospital project are now running their own businesses. So to look ahead another ten years and imagine this community as an Ithaca or a Cambridge for Rwanda is incredibly exciting."

→
A bedroom in the Butaro Doctors' Sharehousing.

Reflecting on the improbable development of the Butaro Hospital and surrounding area, Murphy tells me, "I love that there was a naïve, ambitious, whatever-it-takes attitude in the early years of the hospital—even though at times it would be so stressful and problematic in other ways. We created this beautiful thing very, very cheaply, under severe pressure and ridiculous expectations, and yet it still was completed."

Referring to MASS's subsequent work, Murphy says, "I often wonder nostalgically if we're always trying to repeat that. Each year that we gain more expertise, I wonder if expertise is part of the problem sometimes."

Murphy continues: "We take lessons from Butaro, but the lessons from Butaro are the lessons of hospitals. Period. Hospitals, in my mind, are one of the most profound, fascinating, and, for that reason, challenging types of architecture." He contends, "I think it's a real disservice that we've bifurcated health-care architecture as some subdiscipline of architecture. Health-care architecture teaches us about the way all buildings work, instead of the inverse. It is a great disservice because we're missing the opportunity to make hospitals profound statements about how we want our world to be."

Over the years, Murphy and I have talked about what led him into health-care architecture, normally the province of large firms. The work is rarely distinct from a design standpoint, and it's not exactly the sexy career one might associate with being a Harvard-trained architect. In 2011, at a conference where we were both

speaking, Murphy quietly started to tell me more about his father, whose paint-splattered Poughkeepsie High School Crew sweatshirt he wore for his all-nighters and on that fateful evening when he first met Paul Farmer, and it started to make sense.

For much of Murphy's life, he had watched his dad toil over the upkeep of their historic home in Poughkeepsie, New York. Before deciding to go to architecture school, Murphy was living and working in South Africa, when he received word that his dad was terminally ill. His father was given three weeks to live, prompting Murphy to immediately move home.

"When I was growing up, my father spent every weekend fighting to keep the house alive, for years repainting the clapboard exterior, only to restart just when he seemed about to finish," Murphy explains. "With him suddenly laid up in the hospital, the house was clearly winning. Rotting, leaking, and unfinished, his home untouched would decay alongside him."

Murphy put on his dad's sweatshirt and started in on saving his family's home from its cancer. When he removed some water-damaged plaster on the third floor, it revealed that the bones of their home were beautiful, solid wide plank cedar boards. When he polished the door handles, he found they were solid brass.

Two months in, back at home, Murphy's father started to polish some door handles. He then picked up a brush to repaint the fifty-pane windows wrapping the back porch. At four months after his expiration date, Murphy's father was back on a full work schedule. Returning at 6 p.m. each evening, he would join his son in stripping peeling paint off the radiators and replacing the molding.

By nine months, Murphy's father's hair was coming back, and within a year, their house appeared almost completely restored. With his father then fully in remission, Murphy realized how directly his father's health was aligned with the restoration of their house. "It was quite literally what was keeping him alive. It wasn't the building, I realized, but the process of building that gave us health," Murphy says.

The same week that Murphy donned his dad's sweatshirt and went to hear Farmer speak, his father went into septic shock and went to Memorial Sloan Kettering Cancer Center in Boston for the final time. "It was probably the most profound week of my life," Murphy says.

"When my father finally succumbed to cancer fourteen months later—a full twenty-six months longer than his original prognosis—I realized that my choice to become an architect began with him," Murphy explains. "The gift of those twelve months working together, restoring ourselves and our home, instilled a belief that architecture can actually make us healthier. Buildings are not simply shelters to await certain death, he taught me, but instead the bones that gird our ability to live and the spaces that drive us to survive."

Butaro Hospital

Clients: Rwanda Ministry of Health, www.moh.gov.rw
Partners in Health
www.pih.org

Year completed: 2011

Built Area: 72,000 square feet

Cost (USD): $6,600,000

Butaro Doctors' Housing

Client: Partners in Health
www.pih.org

Year completed: 2012

Built Area: 4,700 square feet

Cost (USD): $340,000

Butaro Cancer Center of Excellence

Client: Partners in Health
www.pih.org

Partner: Rwanda Ministry of Health, www.moh.gov.rw

Year completed: 2013

Built Area: 6,200 square feet

Cost (USD): $300,000

Butaro Doctors' Sharehousing

Client: Brigham and Women's Hospital
www.brighamandwomens.org

Year completed: 2015

Built Area: 6,200 square feet

Cost (USD): $400,000

Design: MASS Design Group
www.massdesigngroup.org

Photography: Iwan Baan
www.iwan.com

↑
**Butaro Doctors'
Sharehousing in the
evening.**

←
**View from above the
Butaro Doctors' Housing
and Sharehousing as fog
settles below the hillside.**

2.
Buildings That Heal

→
GHESKIO Cholera Treatment Center in Port-au-Prince, Haiti, by MASS Design Group and Les Centres GHESKIO; completed in 2015.

PA PAKE
MACHINN
LAA
POLIS

Projects Profiled

Like the Butaro Hospital, the three facilities highlighted in this chapter were created to safeguard one of our most fundamental human needs: health. In a time when some buildings—hospitals included—are known to make us sicker, these buildings restore and nourish.

Leading off, the Angdong Health Center in rural China was created with local labor and materials to provide a unique experience and resource for its community. In a departure from the isolating environment of many hospitals, the project was specifically designed to draw the public in and facilitate connection.

In a very different context, WelcomeHealth, a free clinic in Northwest Arkansas, was designed to make patients feel valued and cared for. The difference is apparent from the moment patients set foot in the building; the beautiful materials and modern furniture look nothing like those of a typical, generic clinic. Employing a veritable army of volunteer professionals, the organization provides free medical and dental services to the uninsured.

From there, we head to Port-au-Prince to a first-of-its-kind cholera treatment center—the result of a unique partnership between MASS Design Group and Haiti's Les Centres GHESKIO. It was born in the wake of the 2010 cholera outbreak, which continues to ravage Haiti. The center not only provides a refuge for terribly sick patients but also treats the water that spreads the disease to prevent further infection.

design for impact
Angdong Health Center

John Lin describes himself as a professional immigrant. Born in Taiwan, at a young age Lin moved with his family to Pittsburgh, Pennsylvania, where his father pursued his doctorate from Carnegie Mellon University. Lin has no memory of it, but he learned years later that when he was a child, his parents took him to see Fallingwater, a nearby house designed by Frank Lloyd Wright. It's an occasion that very well may have planted the seed of Lin's interest in architecture.

Lin spent his teens and twenties in upstate New York and, ultimately, New York City, where he decided to attend art school at The Cooper Union rather than enroll in Yale University's premed program. "That was quite a choice," Lin recalls. "Coming from a traditional Asian American family, it was a big deal to give that up."

After a year in art school, Lin shifted gears and redirected his studies toward medicine, with Cooper Union's engineering program as the foundation. After pursuing that for four years while working in various hospitals, including an internship in New York's St. Vincent's Hospital emergency room, Lin had completed the requirements to enter medical school. On the brink of graduation, he found himself enthralled in an architecture class led by the late Raimund Abraham, an Austrian architect.

"Abraham basically presented architecture as a study of the human condition; it was not about buildings at all. It was about the process of building and what that meant in relationship to the ontological condition of man. It was the sacredness of digging into the earth to build something," Lin explains. "That really captured my imagination; it was exactly what I had always wanted to do."

Lin abruptly switched from studying the human body to studying the human condition through the practice of architecture. He applied to Cooper Union for the third time and, nine years after first entering the school, graduated with his architecture degree.

Upon graduation, Lin relocated to Denmark for two years and then to Hong Kong with his partner, now wife, who is Danish. "We went to Hong Kong on one-way tickets," he admits. "We had no idea what we would do." Once there, though, Lin found a teaching job at the Chinese University of Hong Kong and began undertaking "design/build" projects, in which students both designed and made structures. Most of the projects were artistically motivated or experimental in nature. It was through the university, specifically a design competition it hosted, that Lin ended up with the chance to redesign a primary school in rural China, where his work took root.

"I never intended to do social projects of this type," Lin explains. "It happened along the way and, really, by chance. The process of building is my greatest motivation. That process is both extremely meaningful and increasingly rare. Most people don't ever experience making something the way we get to do in architecture."

While working on that first project, which he described to me as "a rethinking of what a school meant in the village," Lin met a young British architect named Joshua Bolchover. The two embarked on an array of projects and exhibitions together. Then, in 2005, when the Chinese government announced its plan to urbanize half of the remaining 700 million rural citizens by 2030, Lin and Bolchover launched Rural Urban Framework, a nonprofit research initiative within the University of Hong Kong, where they were both on faculty by that point. The nonprofit's relationship with the university covers Lin and Bolchover's time so they can undertake pro bono projects. They are required to do research, so they use that time to build projects that are investigative and innovative.

"We work in areas where there is only generic construction," Lin and Bolchover have written. "Our aim is to make architecture—spaces that go beyond pure utility, and inspire through their experience of light, material, and organization."

←
A woman, girl, and
dog walk near the
center.

↓
A patient pauses as
he walks up the
ramped corridor of
the building.

↘
Patient family
members visit with
the health center
staff.

The Angdong Health Center, completed in 2012, was a collaboration between Rural Urban Framework and the Institute for Integrated Rural Development, Hong Kong (IRD), an organization dedicated to making the transition from rural to urban life easier for Chinese people, particularly those with low incomes.

Much of IRD's work during its first two decades has been focused on education. During that time, IRD came to understand that education and health in the region are deeply interwoven. Students are frequently unable to afford school tuition, especially in the face of rising health costs. Alan Sze, executive director of IRD, explains: "Many of the students in rural China are leaving home and living at more urban schools during the weekdays, forcing them to withdraw from their villages. When a single member in a family has a major illness, the whole family could end up broke."

The Angdong Health Center, a three-story, twenty-bed building in China's Hunan Province, is designed as a gathering place for the community, not just where people go when they are sick. As such, it's more like a community health center than a traditional hospital, though it is staffed by medical professionals and provides a range of care.

Sze, who has long had an appreciation for design, stumbled on Lin and Bolchover's work and reached out to see if they'd be interested in working on the Angdong Health Center. "The work of Rural Urban Framework is very rare, because most Hong Kong architects are heavily involved in the urban settings, such as with property development and commercial projects," Sze explains. "Far fewer venture into the rural area, and even those who do focus on the residential side."

In Lin's eyes, the Angdong Health Center is not just another health facility: "It's about institutional buildings as important investments. This is essentially the beginning of rural institutions—and not only through the buildings but also how they're built and how they're run."

There are major economic disparities between Hong Kong, where Lin and Bolchover are based, and rural China. Luckily, many donors in Hong Kong feel the need to give back to the mainland. The Angdong Health Center, a case in point, benefited from $170,000 in philanthropic contributions.

The role of philanthropic partners is central to Rural Urban Framework's approach, as is partnership in general. "We see development as the integration of government, villagers, village leaders, charities, and others. As shareholders in a community, they are inherently looking beyond very specific projects, like buildings," Lin explains. "That's how we've been able to enter into true dialogue and to see projects not as isolated entities or simply as physical hardware. Schools and hospitals themselves are buildings, but they are much more than that within the larger picture of the development of a community or region."

The health center, in fact, replaced an older hospital on an adjacent site, built with little physical connection to the community. From his premed training, Lin was all too familiar with buildings of the type, which exist the world over: "If you spend time in hospitals, you quickly become aware of how they are very often institutionalized, impersonal machines."

Lin goes on: "Hospitals are theoretically public buildings. Yet so much about hospitals, operationally, is about isolation—isolating patients, isolating people from each other, isolating different kinds of illnesses. It's a weird contradiction."

Rural Urban Framework started the design process for the Angdong Health Center by thinking about the myriad public uses of a hospital. Lin and Bolchover observed people in hospitals. They interviewed people about their hospital experiences. And they began to realize something: the most common behavior in a hospital has historically been the last thing on most architects' minds. Sure, people are healed and heal within a hospital, but the thing people do more than anything else is . . . wait. Wait to see a doctor, wait for a family member or friend, wait on test results.

They began asking themselves, instead of sitting or standing in line, what if people could use the time to walk around for exercise? This question, combined with the need for access to all levels of the building, led to inclusion of a ramp, which became the defining feature of the building.

"Rather than an elevator, we had the idea to make a ramp, as it was exactly the same cost," Lin explains. "By doing the ramp, we were able to provide these other public spaces and create a sort of system that ran from the garden on the ground floor up to the roof—all as an extension of the street. In the process, we were able to open up the hospital."

The ground floor includes the reception area, the clinic, injection rooms, and a pharmacy; the recovery wards are on the upper floors. The phasing strategy necessitated that the existing hospital be kept fully operational until the new building was complete, with the ramp inserted as the final component.

The buildings' facades are made from material recycled from old factories in the region. Lin explains, "The facades on the outside and inside, for me, are deeply symbolic of reaching to the past and also reaching to the future."

Rural Urban Framework worked with a local contractor to innovate on his standard product, the concrete block screens that are ubiquitous across China. "The innovation came when we developed a flexible casting mold that could vary the orientation and distance of extrusion or intrusion of the opening in the middle of the blocks," Lin explains. "Through experimentation, we selected three types for their filtration effect and viewing direction." After the molds were prototyped in Hong Kong, a villager in Angdong fabricated the blocks.

Buildings That Heal

Sze emphasizes that the building is not a traditional hospital but a health center designed to be the epicenter of a lot of distributed care and community-building efforts—similar to the Butaro Hospital, described in the previous chapter, and the GHESKIO Cholera Treatment Center, discussed later in this chapter.

Sze explains, "Our staff members still spend time in villages, organize events, and do home visits. We have to do a combination of things to serve the rural residents' health-care needs. So many of the best doctors and health-care professionals are drawn to more urban areas because of the higher quality of life there."

IRD's original plan was to operate the health center itself, but the region's health bureau maintains a heavy hand from a management standpoint. Sze is far more interested in the health center's impact on the community. "I think the community sees it as something that's really opened their minds and changed the concept about what health care is. People see hospitals as places that are not particularly pleasant—somewhere that a healthy person wouldn't think of going.

"Our building is different," Sze asserts. "It has a very open nature, it has various elements to attract people to go inside, and it seems to welcome you. It is very accessible, and its architectural form is inviting. I think people see it and have a much more positive impression of health care. They also experience something new in terms of the activities."

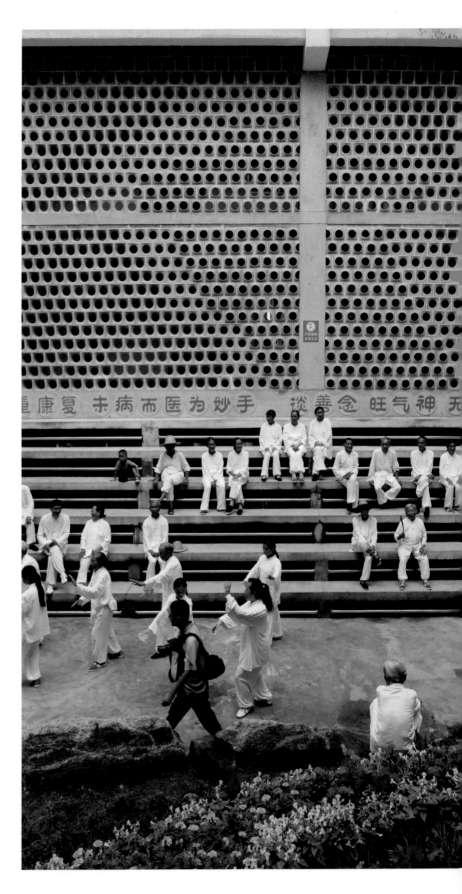

←
A group practices
tai chi in the
courtyard of the
Angdong Health
Center.

↑
Children run up the
ramp leading from
the courtyard.

On the other side of the world from Africa, Lin and Bolchover have unknowingly embraced what MASS Design Group has honed in Rwanda. Rural Urban Framework's website reads: "We hate excess. We revel in low budgets and minimal resources. We work in areas which have limited access to technology, materials or construction expertise. We innovate with what's available: seeking solutions for energy saving, re-use of materials and water collection and filtration."

When I spoke with Lin, he expanded on the idea that limitations are actually conducive to creating dignifying buildings: "One might perceive a lot of what we encountered as architectural limitations—such as a constrained budget or varying quality of materials or construction. But we are able to transform each of them into interesting benefits, and these are exactly the kinds of challenges that we personally like to deal with. We're interested in the kind of value you can give, especially social value. We're also interested in symbolic value. How much can you elevate that? For me, that's the game."

The health center's design is a point of pride for everyone involved. "I think it has definitely brought us a lot of faith in what good architecture can do," Sze explains. "Good architecture can really magnify the impacts; the form brings attention, and the attention helps raise people's expectations. When people's expectations are higher, they will do better, and they will be more receptive to changes."

design for good

← Elevation view of the Angdong Health Center.

→ Light filters into a ramped corridor of the building.

Buildings That Heal

↑
**Children play in the
courtyard of the
health center.**

design for good

Location: Baojing, Xiangxi,
Hunan, China

Year completed: 2012

Built Area: 16,000 square feet

Cost (USD): $300,000

Client:
Institute for Integrated Rural
Development, Hong Kong
www.harvest.org.hk/eng/

Design:
Rural Urban Framework
www.rufwork.org

Photography: Courtesy of
Rural Urban Framework

WelcomeHealth: Northwest Arkansas' Free Health Center

A corridor bisects the
interior of WelcomeHealth,
creating four waiting
rooms finished in red oak.

"This is not what I expected from a free health center."

Monika Fischer-Massie hears this frequently from patients, nurses, and doctors, particularly the first time they walk into her clinic. WelcomeHealth: Northwest Arkansas' Free Health Center serves both the underinsured and uninsured with health and dental care.

There are over one hundred free clinics throughout Arkansas, a state with a population of 3 million. According to the U.S. Department of Health and Human Services, the uninsured rate in Arkansas fell by 46 percent after the Affordable Care Act (ACA) was enacted in 2010, enabling 234,000 Arkansans to gain coverage. Many more residents who would otherwise be uninsured secured coverage through Medicare or related programs as a result of the law. Still, there remains a huge need in the state and beyond, largely filled by free clinics.

"Our attitude is that even people who don't have a lot of money, who are poor or not very well educated, deserve both care and the chance to receive care in a building like this," Fischer-Massie, the director of WelcomeHealth, explains.

The single-story building was once the property of the Washington County Health Department, part of a state agency. It had a brief second life as an exercise center, fell vacant and into disrepair for many years, and ultimately became home to WelcomeHealth. By the time Fischer-Massie and her team found it, the building was little more than a shell, with gym lockers lining two of the walls.

"The only thing I remember from my first visit is that it was really dingy," recalls Fischer-Massie. "I honestly didn't know what to make of it. I didn't have the vision to see something else. Thankfully, our architects had the vision we needed. They could see something that we couldn't even imagine."

WelcomeHealth was designed by Marlon Blackwell Architects, one of the most highly regarded design firms in the United States. Marlon Blackwell, its principal and founder, was born in Fürstenfeldbruck, a U.S. Air Force base in Germany, just outside of Munich. The base is famous for being adjacent to the small airport where eleven Israeli Olympic team members were killed in 1972; at the time, Blackwell was fifteen years old. A quintessential military brat, Blackwell grew up for various amounts of time in the Philippines, Florida, Colorado, and Montana, finally settling in the place he considers home, Arkansas.

Blackwell's early passions were visual but not architectural. "I originally wanted to be a cartoonist," Blackwell tells me. "That's what I did when I got home from school—I created characters and stories and cartoons." He drew a recurring strip for his high school newspaper and, ultimately, while in architecture school at Auburn University.

Still, Blackwell tells me, "I never lived with design; I lived with undesign. Architecture was something that I sort of grew into. It came from a way to interrupt the world as it was presented to me. It became a means of expression. It's really a way of view interpreting your engagement with the world."

Blackwell's firm is well-known for its elegant structures—ranging from a fifty-foot-tall tower house in the woods to a minimalist church converted from an old aluminum-clad garage building and a gymnasium on tribal lands in Oklahoma where a tornado had torn through. But it isn't just elegance that the firm prides itself on; public engagement is a core tenet of the work. "Through both our regular projects and our pro bono work, we try to show how design and civic engagement go together," Blackwell explains.

Blackwell's ethos resonates deeply with that of Fischer-Massie, who also found her way to Arkansas after being born and raised in Germany. Arriving in the United States to study hotel and restaurant management, Fischer-Massie went on to earn her master's degree and doctorate in health science. After working as a professor in Louisiana, she relocated to Fayetteville, where her husband had been living. He was on the board of what was then called the Northwest Arkansas Free Health Center, which is now WelcomeHealth.

With her background in business and education, Fischer-Massie joined the board as well. After the group's executive director retired, the board asked Fischer-Massie if she would take over as director. She declined, but relented two years later, provided it would be a part-time position. That was sixteen years ago, with the position being full-time throughout.

Perhaps the person most surprised by her love for the work is Fischer-Massie herself. "I never imagined myself working in a nonprofit. I always thought I would be great for the corporate world, but it's a good thing I never actually ventured in that direction, because that would not have been the right place for me."

Fischer-Massie now coordinates an army of professionals to serve approximately three thousand people per year. WelcomeHealth has eleven paid employees and more than fifty professional volunteers. Among them are dentists and physicians but also oral surgeons, pharmacists, a psychologist, nurses, diabetes educators, a physical therapist, a speech therapist, a neurologist, a gynecologist, an endocrinologist, and a preventive medicine physician.

It's a remarkable operation and one on which many depend. Yet for years, both the caregivers and those being cared for suffered from an undignifying environment. "WelcomeHealth had great doctors and volunteers but really bad facilities," Blackwell says.

"Our work with Marlon's firm just kept evolving and evolving and evolving," Fischer-Massie explains. "It was just amazing. The most amazing part was to find out how knowledgeable architects have to be in order to create buildings. Beyond their designs, they have to know all the materials and how everything works together."

First and foremost, architects have to be knowledgeable about those who use the spaces they create. Blackwell's firm consulted everyone who used the building—the caregivers and those being cared for—about their experience of it and dreams for it, something that surprised many of them who were used to top-down mandates, not bottom-up design processes.

One thing the designers heard loud and clear was that light was important; the old space had been quite dark. "We have a lot of daylight in the facility now," Fischer-Massie says. "When patients walk in, they get a feeling of health because of the light and materials, which include bright surfaces and lots of wood."

→
Wood-clad waiting rooms
provide a warm contrast
to the bright white
corridor that bisects the
building.
↓
The main axis through the
building leads to a
light-filled community
meeting room.

Blackwell agrees: "We managed to create a warm, inviting place with natural light that just feels, I'll use the word, dignifying." The firm also gave attention to the entry of the building so patients, volunteers, and staff would feel they were entering into a special place. "We wanted them to feel welcome.

"It's probably better than most doctors' offices in the state. The underserved are served very well here. To put a fine point on it, one of the organization's problems was that they were losing a roll or two of toilet paper and paper towels per day in the old space," Blackwell explains, implying they were taken by patients. "Since the new building, they haven't lost anything, not once."

When I asked Blackwell to elaborate on that surprising anecdote, he told me, "It's about respect. We've shown them respect, the folks who we're serving, and they wouldn't dare do that. It's small, but it underscores the power of architecture to strengthen institutions and to enrich people's lives, even subconsciously."

Blackwell doesn't sugarcoat the work. "Design-wise, we put a lot into this building. But we also didn't lose money on the project; we ultimately got a decent fee, once the organization secured a grant. The motivation was never that fee; it was the opportunity to do something to help."

The design has absolutely helped to distinguish WelcomeHealth. Fischer-Massie often hears visiting doctors say, "My office is not as beautiful as your office." A particular point of pride for her is that WelcomeHealth is now the only health-care facility in Northwest Arkansas that is LEED certified, referring to the U.S. Green Building Council's Leadership in Energy and Environmental Design program. The LEED program actually has more to do with the energy performance of a building than the aesthetic design, which visitors no doubt see first.

With the firm's help, WelcomeHealth partnered with an architecture class at the University of Arkansas to fulfill the requirements for LEED certification, which is often a time-consuming and costly endeavor.

When asked what she would tell her peers in related organizations, Fischer-Massie is quick to talk again about the importance of light. "I've seen many free clinics, and very few have any daylight at all. I think that's absolutely critical because light projects health."

WelcomeHealth: Northwest Arkansas' Free Health Center

Location: Fayetteville, Arkansas, United States

Year completed: 2013

Built Area: 9,700 square feet

Cost (USD): $630,000

Client: WelcomeHealth
www.welcomehealthnwa.org

Design:
Marlon Blackwell Architects
www.marlonblackwell.com

Photography: Timothy Hursley
www.timothyhursley.com

↑
Immediately inside the
front doors are two
waiting areas, with one
containing the reception
desk and the other the
pharmacy.

design
for
resilience

GHESKIO
Cholera
Treatment
Center

↙
Perforated steel
panels enclosing the
GHESKIO Cholera
Treatment Center,
made by local
craftspeople,
welcome light and
aid ventilation.

Just a few minutes before 5 p.m. on January 12, 2010, the island nation of Haiti was struck by a devastating 7.0 magnitude earthquake. The epicenter was just sixteen miles west of Haiti's most populated city, its capital, Port-au-Prince. Estimates vary, but approximately 150,000–300,000 people died and millions more were affected. Countless homes, along with school, government, and hospital buildings, collapsed.

A prominent spokesperson for Haiti's health system after the earthquake, Dr. Vanessa Rouzier, worked with the U.S. Department of Health and Human Services to provide emergency care to over 3,000 trauma victims. The nongovernmental organization (NGO) she works for, Les Centres GHESKIO (short for "Haitian Group for the Study of Kaposi's Sarcoma and Opportunistic Infections"), converted its three-acre campus into a tent city for more than 10,000 people. All the while, Rouzier fought to maintain the organization's regular lifesaving services.

"There we were, trying to reestablish some sort of normalcy after the earthquake, and then, ten months later, we got struck with the deadliest cholera outbreak in recent times," Rouzier recalls.

Earthquakes were relatively common in Haiti. Cholera—an infectious and often fatal bacterial disease of the small intestine—was not. Its symptoms include severe vomiting and diarrhea. Capitalizing on the region's compromised water infrastructure since the earthquake, the waterborne disease spread like wildfire.

"In the beginning, it was very overwhelming and extremely scary because it was a new disease; people were not familiar with it. In our training, doctors are taught about cholera, but we had no practice or experience with it," explains Rouzier. GHESKIO, whose badly damaged campus was still being rebuilt after the earthquake, promptly erected a tent to serve as a makeshift cholera treatment center. Beyond accepting patients, the organization had to train staff and educate the community about the signs and symptoms of cholera.

"The outbreak was massive. People were literally being brought in by wheelbarrow. We were flooded with patients," Rouzier says. Of the makeshift tent, she tells me: "It worked, in the sense that we were able to provide care for patients immediately." The tent held upward of one hundred patients at a time, all requiring constant monitoring and support.

"There were also many limitations to the tent," Rouzier explains. "It was cramped and very hot. You can imagine in the summer, when it's 36 degrees Celsius [nearly 100 degrees Fahrenheit], it can be stifling with no ventilation system. Our patients were actually getting dehydrated from the heat, not just their cholera symptoms."

The severe limitations of the tent soon gave way to discussions with MASS Design Group and other partners about the need for a more permanent structure. Even if the cholera outbreak could be contained, it would take years to eradicate the disease. What was needed was an actual treatment center, with proper ventilation, light, and waste management. Key among these is the management of human waste, which can contaminate the water and further spread the disease.

When the cholera outbreak first unfolded, MASS was hard at work on a new tuberculosis hospital in Port-au-Prince in partnership with GHESKIO, as the previous hospital had been ruined in the earthquake. The project came to MASS through a doctor named Serena Koenig, who knew of MASS from work she had done with Partners in Health before joining GHESKIO. Koenig's boyfriend and future husband, Mark Tompkins, was a real estate developer. He combined his sense of space and his number-crunching skills to design a needed TB hospital for GHESKIO, using a popular spreadsheet program.

Looking for feedback, Koenig had sent the sketch to Alan Ricks, cofounder and chief operating officer of MASS, who couldn't quite believe what he was looking at when he saw it. "It was amazing. Mark even poshéd the walls and had a range of line weights, as architectural plans do. In many ways, it was really impressive." While the plan for the L-shaped building included a courtyard and was commendable in other respects, its strict rectilinear shape focused exclusively on function at the expense of form.

Ricks flew to Port-au-Prince the next month, in the fall of 2010, mere weeks before the cholera outbreak came to light. As work on the TB hospital got under way, the need for a facility to aid GHESKIO's cholera work quickly became apparent. MASS began to discuss the challenges GHESKIO was facing, the most important being contaminated human waste and lack of durability of the tents.

Back-of-the-envelope estimates projected that a huge sum of money would be required to maintain GHESKIO's temporary facilities over the many years it would take to eradicate the outbreak. A permanent facility, which could be used for different purposes in the future, made good economic sense. Ricks explains, "With a permanent facility, we knew we could deal with the waste control situation, make a more comfortable environment for the patients and caregivers, and create a more dignifying space."

Already stretched and unprepared for the expense, GHESKIO didn't have funds on hand for the proposed cholera treatment center. So the organization and MASS partnered on a Clinton Global Initiative commitment—part of the Clinton Foundation's annual meeting—using the association and publicity to unite a cohort of donors to fund the construction. MASS, itself a nonprofit, committed to designing the building pro bono and also took responsibility for raising the capital construction cost of $800,000.

→
A large fan moves air through the center.

↓
Health workers carry a treatment chair into the center.

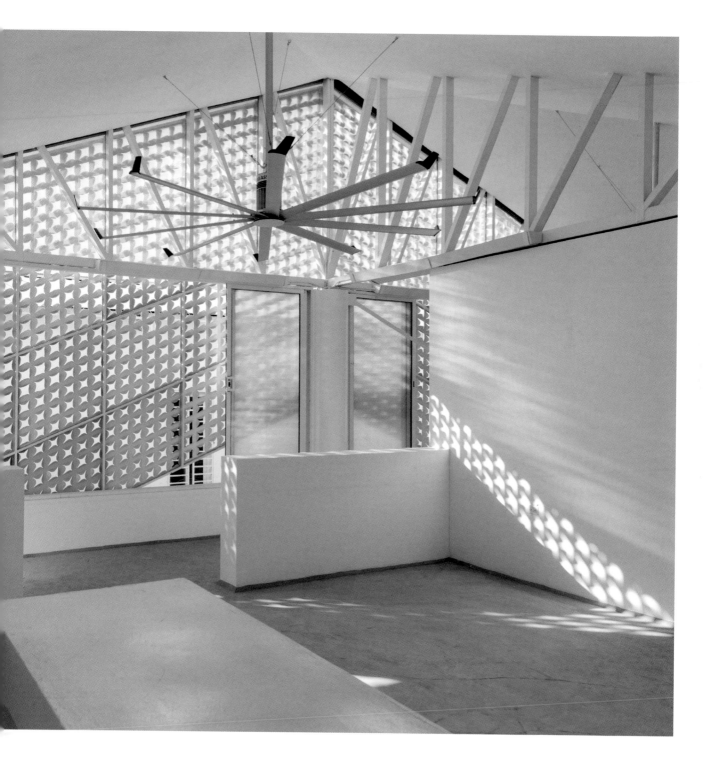

Buildings That Heal

Had either Rouzier or Ricks ever imagined being involved in this kind of work when they entered medical school and architecture school, respectively?

"Absolutely not," Rouzier quickly replies. "I don't think anybody imagines where you end up; I don't think there is any way I could see clearly what I would do after fifteen years of schooling." A native of Port-au-Prince, Rouzier attended college at Loyola University New Orleans and then medical school at McGill University in Montreal, where she completed her residency in pediatrics and a fellowship in infectious diseases.

"I knew that I wanted to come back to Haiti and to give back to the community for having been blessed with so much," Rouzier explains, but she hadn't even heard of GHESKIO until shortly before her return. In 2009, the organization's well-known founder, Dr. Jean William Pape, welcomed her home and to GHESKIO, shortly before the earthquake struck.

For his part, Ricks had once debated between pursuing a career as a surgeon and becoming an architect. Born in San Antonio, Texas, he was raised in Dallas, attended college in Colorado, and then moved out east to pursue his architecture degree from the Harvard Graduate School of Design.

"When I started architecture school, I was caught completely off-guard by what we did during our first semester," Ricks laments. "It had almost nothing to do with what I thought architecture would be. It was hard to appreciate how that could have any application that would positively affect anybody." He continues, "It was abstract, academic, and highly theoretical," echoing what other designers interviewed for this book told me about their education.

Yet it was at Harvard that Ricks met and started working with a small group of classmates to cofound MASS Design Group. Their late night and weekend extracurricular work on what is now the acclaimed Butaro Hospital, highlighted in chapter 1, became a defining moment for him. "I still think I learned a lot in grad school and that design pedagogy is meaningful as a way of interrogating problems and thinking about things in a different way. What was missing was the application: where do we turn this into something that can improve people's lives?" For Ricks and his peers, the Butaro Hospital became that opportunity.

Ricks describes the tuberculosis hospital that they were originally in Haiti to build with GHESKIO as the first real opportunity that he and MASS had to apply what they had learned via the Butaro Hospital. Specifically, Butaro was a proof of concept for the link between airborne infections and ventilation that the MASS cofounders had hypothesized with Professor Edward Nardell of the Harvard T.H. Chan School of Public Health. The work had direct relevance to the TB hospital, and ventilation was a top priority, even if not from an airborne disease standpoint, for the GHESKIO Cholera Treatment Center.

Long before the earthquake and the cholera outbreak, Haiti was subject to extreme instability, both economically and politically. It is often cited as the poorest country in the Western Hemisphere, and it had experienced a highly contentious presidential election around the time of the two catastrophes.

Ricks reminds me that Dr. Paul Farmer, cofounder of Partners in Health, which also works extensively in Haiti, describes this kind of condition as "acute on chronic." It's a situation in which a community has chronic systemic problems that are exacerbated by an acute event, be it natural, like the earthquake, or man-made, like cholera. "It's been decades of acute on chronic events and perpetual instability in Haiti," Ricks continues, "and then many of the interventions from international organizations have further problematized things.

"Ironically, it was a very difficult place to work compared with Rwanda, which had a booming economy and an efficient government used to taking agency," Ricks explains. "In Haiti, there's actually a strong construction industry, including a lot of architects. There was a lot more expertise but also a high level of corruption and entrenched ways of getting things done.

"You had a flood of NGOs coming in, promising to solve all of Haiti's problems," Ricks recalls of the time. "Not to overly generalize, but the reason so few of those projects have been successful is naïveté about the way Haiti operates."

By contrast, in Ricks's assessment, since its founding in the early 1980s, GHESKIO had built trust and a network of allies throughout the country: "They're Haitian, and they've been there for decades. They are well connected and have a long history of making every effort to get along with whoever is in power so that they can be effective. I think that really enabled us; otherwise we would have been lost."

↑
**The interior of the center
is light and breezy.**

GHESKIO's broad mission includes maternal and child health and nutrition, provision of clean water and sanitation, primary education, vocational training, and microfinance programs. In partnership with the medical school at Cornell University, it provides care, free of charge, to a target community of 60,000 surrounding its campus. But many others come from far and wide, and the organization has a policy of never turning anyone away.

Rouzier serves as head of pediatrics and nutrition at GHESKIO, supervising the largest pediatric HIV clinic in the Caribbean. In general, she and her team care for vulnerable populations including pregnant women, infants, children, and adolescents. It was already a herculean task before the earthquake and cholera.

In 2015, Rouzier set foot for the first time in the finished GHESKIO Cholera Treatment Center building that Ricks and his team at MASS designed in partnership with the organization. "There was a clear sense of awe," Rouzier recalls. "It's big, bright, and airy."

The functionality of the center impresses Rouzier the most, starting with the spatial setup. "When you have a cholera treatment center, you have very sick patients, all of whom you need to be able to visualize at the same time," Rouzier explains. "You have to be on your toes when you're treating cholera patients because they need minute-by-minute supervision. The new center has this open common room where the two or three nurses who are on service can quickly eyeball everybody.

"It's also really well ventilated," Rouzier says with palpable relief. "I think that's one of the most satisfying things. The intense heat that we endured under the tents is gone. It's really breezy and comfortable for the patients, as well as for our staff. You walk in and it literally feels cool, even when it's blazing hot outside in the summer. You feel like you've walked into an oasis."

The center is naturally lit—another contrast to the dark tents—a crucial feature, Rouzier emphasizes, for periods when the facility or area is without electricity.

Perhaps the greatest innovation is the facility's on-site water treatment system, eliminating the need for waste removal, which is both dangerous and costly. The treatment takes two forms. The first is water catchment: rainwater is funneled into cisterns below the building, which feed the sinks and toilets and provide potable water for drinking, crucial hydration for the patients. The rainwater catchment also mitigates flooding, a problem the campus previously suffered regularly.

The other form of water treatment is a biodigester, which enables the center to dispose of and treat human waste compromised with cholera without risk of contaminating the environment. "We found that there were fundamental infrastructural failures that create an environment that cholera exploits," Ricks explains, specifically referring to water management. All told, the GHESKIO Cholera Treatment Center can treat up to 250,000 gallons of water annually.

The need for ventilation drove the creation of the building's distinctive screens, which line the exterior, painted in a chorus of blues. "We needed to design a building that could breathe but that GHESKIO could also lock down during a hurricane," Ricks explains. "More specifically, we wanted to have something that would be very porous under most conditions while being equipped with operable solid panels on the inside that could be closed."

Privacy from the bustling street life just outside the building was another factor. Ricks and his team asked themselves, "How do we create privacy, ensure good ventilation, and provide adequate shading so that we're not heating this space up?"

A MASS colleague named Nathan King had experience in developing customized screens, so Ricks enlisted his help. "Nathan had used a robot to make highly customized patterns, so we used the same scripting to create the design that optimized all these different degrees of openings, based on what we were trying to achieve with ventilation and privacy."

The challenge then became how to build it. MASS could most easily have had the screens fabricated in the United States and shipped to Haiti. "It would have been totally possible, but we were inspired by a couple of things that we saw locally," Ricks recalls. The first was a rich history of artistry and craftsmanship in metalworking. Haiti is well-known for its artwork, most frequently stemming from recycled oil drums that artisans unroll and then chisel, cut, and hammer into wall decorations—they're seen all over the world.

"We were inspired by the capabilities of the metalworkers to do really detailed, customized work. We were also inspired by the playfulness and the colorfulness of their work," Ricks explains. "We wondered, how do we take this condition that threatens to rob cholera patients of their dignity and bring that back into the project a little bit?"

Ricks, King, and their team developed the design for the screens and created exact-scale templates that artisans then used to etch out the panels, each of which is unique. The artisans produced an array of jigs for all the different apertures that needed to be cut and pried open.

Beyond the screens, MASS worked with local craftspeople, including GHESKIO's own staff, to fabricate not just the cabinetry and woodwork for the facility but also the beds and chairs where patients are diagnosed and treated. In the old tents, GHESKIO had used army cots with a hole cut in the middle for placement of a bucket to measure the amount of feces. "That's how you determine cholera," Ricks explains.

The cots inevitably would rip and have to be thrown away because it was impossible to replace just the fabric. So MASS created a new, adjustable bed frame with removable pads that could be sanitized and maintained. MASS also designed new chairs to be used for initial diagnoses; making do with what it had, GHESKIO had previously cut jagged holes in fiberglass school chairs for that purpose.

↑
Local craftspeople cut steel
sheets in patterns to allow
light and air to flow through
while ensuring privacy.

Since the GHESKIO Cholera Treatment Center opened, in mid-2015, it has documented just one new case of cholera in its target community of 60,000 people. "You have to understand that's tremendous, considering that the living conditions of the people haven't changed," Rouzier reminds me. The building is no doubt a contributor, as are the community education and vaccines offered by the organization.

Throughout this time, however, the center has been full of patients from other parts of Port-au-Prince and from Haiti more broadly. Going back to its early days, before the new center, Rouzier tells me, "We have never closed—not one day or even one hour—since 2010. The center operates twenty-four hours a day, seven days a week.

"People know to come to us if they have diarrhea. We tell people they have to chlorinate their water, and we've promoted cleaning of the slum areas," Rouzier continues. "Even though many people still don't have access to latrines, we've been able to control cholera."

GHESKIO and Haiti saw a decline in cases over several years, but since 2014, cholera has been on the rise again. In 2015, more than 25,000 cases were reported throughout Haiti, an increase over the year before, and that number was surpassed in 2016. Rouzier emphasizes that those figures account only for the cases that are reported, but they are clearly rising.

"The battle is not over, and there is still a lot of work to be done," Rouzier reminds me. "We can't afford to lose momentum when cholera is out of sight, out of mind. It's not in the news as much and people kind of forget about it, but it is still one of the largest outbreaks."

In August 2016, after years of silence and denials, the United Nations accepted responsibility for the cholera outbreak. Its origins were traced to a UN base, home to peacekeepers from Nepal. The base abuts a tributary of the Artibonite River, the longest and most important river in Haiti.

Since the original outbreak in 2010, more than 700,000 Haitians had become ill with cholera, with over 9,000 reported deaths. Still, were it not for the carefully coordinated response by partners such as GHESKIO and the Ministry of Health, the losses could have been far greater. In many respects, that coordination has been a model of effective intervention, and the GHESKIO Cholera Treatment Center has been a beacon in otherwise dark times.

GHESKIO Cholera Treatment Center

Location: Port-au-Prince, Haiti

Year completed: 2015

Built Area: 7,500 square feet

Cost (USD): $800,000

Client: Les Centres GHESKIO
www.gheskio.org

Design: MASS Design Group
www.massdesigngroup.org

Photography: Iwan Baan
www.iwan.com

↑
**Evening view of the
GHESKIO Cholera
Treatment Center.**

Buildings That Heal

3.
Shelter for the Soul

→
St. Jerome's Centre in Nakuru, Kenya, by Orkidstudio and St. Jerome's Centre; completed in 2014.

Projects Profiled

Something can be called "home" but never actually put one at ease. On the other hand, to have a place of comfort and consistency in a life that has otherwise been lacking in both can be transformative. This is what James Baldwin was getting at when he wrote: "Perhaps home is not a place but simply an irrevocable condition." This chapter looks at three places that create a sense of home, both literally and in terms of the "irrevocable condition" that Baldwin wisely identified.

The Cottages at Hickory Crossing are a cluster of houses for fifty of the most chronically homeless people in Dallas, Texas. The creation of the nonprofit design firm bcWORKSHOP and a broad array of partners, the fully furnished cottages provide community and stability for some of the city's most vulnerable.

From Dallas we head to rural Kenya, where Orkidstudio worked with a community to build a home for orphaned children. The St. Jerome's Centre exudes warmth, love, and life. The building's colorful spaces lift the spirits of neglected and forgotten children, making them feel valued.

Back in the United States, against great odds, Michael Maltzan Architecture joined forces with Skid Row Housing Trust on the Star Apartments. Partnering with the city to provide on-site supportive services, the building pushes the boundaries of the city's building code as only the second prefabricated housing development in Los Angeles.

The Cottages at Hickory Crossing

In the shadow of downtown Dallas's gleaming skyscrapers sits a cluster of fifty small cottages that one might expect to find on the cover of *Dwell* magazine. The tenants are not the young professionals whom cities such as New York and San Francisco target in their marketing of "micro housing," small one-room apartments. Instead, these cottages—each an architectural gem in its own right—were built for the fifty most chronically homeless people in Dallas. For both the residents and the members of the wide-ranging team who built it, the path to this community was a long and challenging one.

Cities across the country, and around the world, have long wrestled with how to address homelessness, often imposing rules without addressing the root causes, such as displacement caused by gentrification, unemployment, mental illness, and addiction. More than a decade ago, in 2006, the City of Dallas passed an ordinance making it illegal for homeless people to sleep in public places. Those who did were subject to fines, arrests, and jail time. With upward of six hundred chronically homeless people in the area, and few places to go, the ordinance made life all the more difficult and complicated for those on the street.

At the time, a local church, First Presbyterian Church of Dallas, was among many to respond. Offering up the church's parking lot on its own property, the pastor effectively circumvented the ordinance. For months on end, those with no other place to go—sometimes fifty or sixty people per night—arrived each evening with their few worldly possessions. Thin scraps of cardboard afforded a small amount of comfort on the cold concrete and hard asphalt. The church brought in a portable toilet and hired a security guard to help keep the peace.

The image of people sleeping in that parking lot remains seared in architect Brent Brown's memory. He was not only a member of the church but also an architect, and housing was among his specialties. "I was very disappointed that I wasn't able to garner the time and focus to try and bring a more dignified solution," he tells me years later. "It has always kind of haunted me."

Brown is a Texan's Texan. He was born in rural Longview, a couple of hours' drive east of Dallas, and raised in the area. He remembers watching his parents work in the oil and gas industries. "There were engineering aspects to my parents' work—what I would call creative solutions to pragmatic issues in the field," Brown recalls. "It wasn't exactly design, and in my youth I never would have talked about it that way."

Years later, in tandem with his private practice as an architect, Brown founded a nonprofit organization called bcWORKSHOP, short for "Building Community Workshop." He did so around the time of Dallas's homeless ordinance. Brown enlisted his organization's first cohort of AmeriCorps VISTA volunteers—part of a yearlong domestic service program—to undertake a project during a day of service honoring Dr. Martin Luther King Jr. They called it "5750," which was the number of documented homeless individuals in Dallas at the time.

The bcWORKSHOP crew constructed a series of public installations throughout the city to raise awareness and draw attention to the issue. They pointed out the cruelty, not to mention dysfunction, of the city's panhandling ordinances by erecting wooden cutouts of families and individuals with cardboard signs bearing quotations from Dr. King about dignity and respect. Other signs said things like "The price of a Super Bowl ticket will house a homeless person for two years."

"We were trying to poke at popular culture and, at the same time, the regulatory constraints that had been put into place around panhandling or soliciting along major roadways," Brown explains.

↑
Aerial view of The Cottages at Hickory Crossing site.

At the time, Brown's firm and bcWORKSHOP shared office space with Central Dallas Community Development Corporation. The building, an old department store warehouse, was nestled in Dallas's Deep Ellum neighborhood, known as the city's music district. The space itself was long and narrow, split the long way, straight down the middle. On one side were Brown and his enterprises, and on the other was Central Dallas CDC.

"We all sat across from one another," recalls John Greenan, Central Dallas CDC's director. "It was really a great experience, with a lot of cross learning between our people and theirs." There is a lot to be learned from Greenan, a native of Traverse City, Michigan, and a transplant to Dallas, who has degrees in English and law. "I ended up deciding that I liked building housing more than I liked practicing law," says Greenan, explaining his role.

Community development corporations exist in every city across the country and play a critical role in housing, particularly for low-income people in struggling neighborhoods. They are structured as nonprofits and often get involved in economic development, community organizing, and advocacy with real estate developers, among much else.

All told, Greenan and Central Dallas CDC own and operate over 600 units, including a mix of affordable and senior housing and a fifteen-story mixed-use high-rise, where Greenan and his family live. The city has seen a steady rise in housing costs, leaving many behind and making the work of Central Dallas CDC all the more important.

Brown and Greenan often had conversations about the most cutting-edge solutions in housing. In the aftermath of Hurricane Katrina in New Orleans, they watched as tiny houses became a popular alternative to the trailers provided by the Federal Emergency Management Agency, and they wondered about a potential application in Dallas. They also followed a national movement called Housing First with great interest.

The theory behind Housing First is that a home can provide a base of stability from which formerly homeless people can seek out services to rebuild their lives and avoid returning to the street. Cities across the United States as wide-ranging as Anchorage and Atlanta, Salt Lake City and Philadelphia have employed Housing First principles with measurable success. Take Salt Lake City, for example, which reduced its number of chronically homeless people by 91 percent, from nearly 2,000 in 2005 to fewer than 200 in 2015. Brown and Greenan had a hunch that they could combine the two insights from elsewhere and do something groundbreaking in Dallas.

When the Dallas-based W.W. Caruth, Jr. Foundation expressed interest in funding a model community for people experiencing homelessness, Brown and Greenan jumped at the chance to explore their hunch. Greenan explains, "We wanted to show that we can house people who have been homeless, reduce costs, and also have something that the community can be proud of."

The possibility of this project becoming a model—first and foremost for other parts of Dallas—inspired the Caruth Foundation. Monica Smith, senior director of strategic philanthropy at the Communities Foundation of Texas, explains, "If we could serve these most difficult people and do it effectively—not just for the individuals who would be living in the units, but also to show the taxpayer benefits and the cost savings to the system—then other projects would have an easier time getting off the ground."

Before plunging ahead with the cottage concept, bcWORKSHOP sought input from formerly homeless people. There were two key findings from their focus groups and interviews, according to Brown. The first was that people really saw the door itself, and even the key that opened that door, as a symbol of dignity. Having an individual unit, as opposed to a unit in a larger building, sounded downright luxurious to people, a true point of pride.

Residents were craving privacy and security. "To put it simply, what people wanted was control," explains Greenan, "and their own place that they could lock up. Many have had very little control over their lives, and what they wanted was something that would give them that sense."

The second key finding was that people didn't feel that the hallways typical of most low-income housing were conducive to creating community or identity. "It's really difficult to create a sense of home using double-loaded corridors, which are often so sterile and stripped of identity," Brown explains. "You can deal with it with colors and textures

and light and such things, but at the end of the day it ends up being a series of doors, lined up one after the next."

To Brown, that experience of walking down a hallway in an apartment building is underwhelming and even problematic, compared with the experience of walking down a street with the ability to see life around and even inside of houses and buildings. "You may not be able to see everything that's going on in there, but there's a connection internally and externally to what's happening that just doesn't manifest in apartment block developments," Brown explains.

What Brown and the partners created is more like a village. Each little home is a 400-square-foot space including a kitchen with a cooktop, sink, and full refrigerator, along with a bedroom and an accessible full bathroom. Residents may choose to cook for themselves, or they may go over to the 3,000-square-foot community building, where there is a kitchen that was designed with group meals in mind.

The cottages were built by a contractor, as most buildings are. Brown had hoped they might employ some homeless people, but it didn't work out because of the scheduling and ultimate rush to get the project built once it was approved and funds were in place.

At least two people who worked on the project had experienced homelessness, according to Brown. "Their own personal agency got them there," he concedes, "rather than a formalized program or something that would have helped. There were definitely conversations about it; those things are so hard to pull off in the end with any success. With the

project being so long and drawn out, there was a point where I think people were just saying 'Let's just get this thing built.'"

The biggest challenge along the way was figuring out the financing. The project team went down several different paths unsuccessfully, including applying for state tax credits for low-income housing and permanent supportive housing. They also considered a social impact bond, which is contingent on specific outcomes being achieved, most often with a goal of public sector savings. Ultimately, even though it was decided to forgo a social impact bond, the county and city governments were willing to put money in because the team was able to show that if the project succeeded, the local governments would experience significant cost savings.

Another challenge was the process of collaborating with half a dozen different entities. Eventually, the Caruth Foundation saw that the team wasn't moving as quickly as anyone would have liked, and it brought in the Corporation for Supportive Housing as a convener. Greenan felt this was key: "There's an old saying, 'When everybody is in charge, nobody is in charge.' I think you need to establish somebody as a convener or a lead organization or something like that to keep things moving forward."

The fifty residents who now live in the cottages were identified through homeless care providers such as Metro Dallas Homeless Alliance and The Bridge. Most moved in at the end of 2016. They are considered tenants and sign the standard Texas lease form that almost every apartment complex in the state uses. Housing choice vouchers from the Dallas Housing Authority require the tenants to pay 30 percent of any income they have toward the rent.

The work ahead is to measure the project's impact, both on individual residents (Do their mental and physical health and employment prospects improve?) and on the system as a whole (What kind of money can be saved without these folks cycling in and out of services?). Lots of support systems are in place to help achieve those goals. The cottage community is staffed by CitySquare, a Dallas-area nonprofit that provides food, health, housing, and outreach services to the poor. The community is located across the street from the CitySquare Opportunity Center, which offers job training and other support services.

For Brown, the time he's invested in the project has felt like a way of overcoming that helplessness he felt all those years ago while walking by the church parking lot filled with people: "It's so silly. I think I felt like I didn't know enough. We all really have to figure out a way to act in those moments."

Greenan is proud of the work, but he is most excited for the residents: "I hope they feel proud to have a place of their own, relieved to be off the street, and much more secure than where they were living before."

Shelter for the Soul

One such resident is Gregory Philen. A native of Brownwood, some 500 miles southwest of Dallas, Philen says of his new home: "It's just unreal. I call it a blessing, or really a miracle."

That miracle comes to Philen, age fifty-five, after many difficult years of being chronically homeless. After working for nine years doing maintenance for the school district in his hometown, Philen was laid off. He then spent the better part of thirty years drifting from town to town, struggling with alcoholism. For about five years, he worked for United Van Lines, during which time he slept in the cab of the truck when the driver went home each night.

"I felt totally lost," Philen tells me of the decades that he was homeless. "I had a void so big inside of me. I just was empty."

Philen went through almost a dozen treatment centers for alcoholism. He would start to recover, and then life would get hard and he would relapse. In 2015, roughly a year before The Cottages at Hickory Crossing were completed, Philen entered a program run by CitySquare, which ultimately led him to the cottages.

When he arrived, with little more than the clothes on his back, he found his cottage fully furnished, including a television set, a full-size refrigerator, and a range of small comforts including a toothbrush and a slow cooker. Philen was beyond touched. "I feel like it's a home. I don't even look at it like an apartment or anything like that. It's like my own little house here," he says. "They let us be ourselves and do the right things. We have Alcoholics Anonymous meetings, and I now spend a lot of my time trying to help others."

"Every day, I wake up and just thank the Lord above for giving me another chance at life. It's been real good for me," Philen says. "I know it's been good for others here, too. We have classes or meetings every Tuesday and Friday. We just go do what we call 'coffee talk.' Most everybody in the community comes. You don't have to, though. They pretty much leave us alone and let us live like it's just a regular neighborhood."

The Cottages at Hickory Crossing

Location: Dallas, Texas, United States

Year completed: 2016

Built Area: 25,000 square feet

Cost (USD): $6.8 million

Client: Central Dallas Community Development Corporation, www.centraldallascdc.org

Partners: Central Dallas Ministries Metrocare Services www.metrocareservices.org Metro Dallas Homeless Alliance, www.mdhadallas.org University of Texas Southwestern Medical Center www.utsouthwestern.edu Dallas County Criminal Justice System, www.dallascounty.org

Design: bcWORKSHOP www.bcworkshop.org

Photography: Skyler Fike, Leah Jones

Exterior view
of cottages.

Shelter for the Soul

design
for
security
St. Jerome's
Centre

design for good

Light filters into a
corridor through the
wood slat screens.

"When I was young and I saw an airplane in the sky, I used to follow it until I got tired or it disappeared," says Solomon Gatheca. "When I discovered that it was a flying machine and driven by a person, I said, 'I will try to do that.' I will become a pilot."

Now eighteen, Gatheca spent many years of his youth sleeping on the streets of Nakuru, the fourth-largest city in Kenya. "It was hard, horrible. I had to beg for money. I often had no food," Gatheca explains. "There were many cold nights," he adds. Nakuru is one of the highest-elevation areas in Kenya, some six thousand feet above sea level.

Gatheca's dream of becoming a pilot drives him: "I study hard in school. Then, I will go to Nairobi University. After that, I want to work for British Airways."

Gatheca is one of thirty children who live in the St. Jerome's Centre, a children's house on the outskirts of Nakuru. Differing from the vast majority of African orphanages, it was designed as a home by Orkidstudio. Rather than the more customary barrack-style sleeping wards, it has bedrooms limited to four children each. Constructed with a combination of packed earth bags, brick, and wood, St. Jerome's is a refuge for the children who live there, a place filled with color and joy.

"I love it, I just love it," Gatheca says, speaking of the house and also his room. "I watch the sunrise out my window every day."

James Mitchell, the founder of Orkidstudio, lives in Nairobi but was born just south of London and raised near Glasgow. "I grew up in a very creative household, out in the middle of nowhere," he says. "We lived in the woodlands, in this old gamekeeper's house. I spent my life away from TV and video games, climbing trees and building shelters.

"I loved art, and I grew up wanting to be an artist, not an architect," Mitchell continues, "but eventually I decided art was too self-reflective, and I wanted to have a bit more impact. Even at a young age, I think in my mid-teens, I started to think about impact. And then architecture came into my consciousness."

While in architecture school, Mitchell reveled in considering the philosophical implications of design, but he never abandoned his interest in impact. When Mitchell was just nineteen, he and Julissa Kiyenje, a friend from Uganda, ambitiously raised a bit of money, and Mitchell felt confident that he was handy enough to start building. They headed down to Kiyenje's native Uganda to start their first project, a kitchen and communal space for the New Hope for Africa orphanage and school in the Mukono District, near Uganda's capital city, Kampala.

Mitchell says he and Kiyenje quickly realized that they "didn't know how to build foundations, didn't know how to build a slab or do much else. I don't think it dawned on us how little we knew until we got down there. We went and got a local engineer from the community, and we just found a bunch of guys—enough to build. We learned literally everything from them."

Mitchell and his cofounder returned home humbled but determined. In the United Kingdom they registered as a charity, which at the time was the only vehicle they knew of to undertake that sort of work. They called it Orkidstudio, inspired by their first project, an orphanage, though the work would quickly extend to other project types.

Through a family friend of Mitchell, Orkidstudio was soon asked to design an art center to be run by one of the largest children's organizations in Bolivia. "We were getting heavily praised after our first project in Uganda. I was twenty, and I had, I guess, a bit of arrogance, as some twenty-year-olds do," Mitchell explains.

Adding to his confidence, Mitchell had moved to Tokyo to work for Japanese architect Shigeru Ban, perhaps one of the most celebrated designers to make humanitarian causes a defining part of his practice.

"There I was in Tokyo, working for this big architect. I decided, in all my infinite wisdom, to design this building, the art center, for this country that I'd never been to, for this community that I had never met," Mitchell continues. "Suffice to say, when I reached Bolivia, things didn't quite pan out as I had imagined. To be really blunt, I forgot all the good lessons that I had learned from that first project in Uganda." The art center project that had been expected to take three and a half months to complete took more than a year.

The art center stands today, is well used, and hasn't had any major maintenance issues, according to Mitchell. "It all worked out, but the journey to get there was just horrible. Not with the client—we have a great relationship with them still—but just within ourselves and our own team. We argued and we pulled in different directions, we got a lot of things wrong, and we had a lot of tears on the project. But it really taught me so much; I think it was the biggest learning curve of my life. I've always been a pretty confident person, and I came off that project feeling rock bottom. It was maybe a bad place to be, but, in hindsight, a good place to be."

Shelter for the Soul

The opportunity to build the St. Jerome's Centre in Nakuru came to Orkidstudio through word of mouth, this time via one of Mitchell's aunts in the United Kingdom. The group's original building was in a high-crime area of Nakuru and had been broken into. St. Jerome's didn't own the land. The staff knew that new facilities were needed, but they didn't know where to start.

In more traditional orphanages that Mitchell visited, he didn't see spaces for kids to develop, an observation affirmed during their conversations with the kids. So he and the team eyed limiting the size of rooms: "We wanted to create a range of spaces—small reading spaces or areas for kids to play in on their own time, as well as bigger areas, like a football pitch."

At about 65 feet wide and 650 feet deep, the site itself is disproportionately long and narrow. The St. Jerome's staff wanted to be near the road, but they also needed to be able to get agricultural vehicles to the back of the site. The result is two buildings slightly staggered in a V shape, which has benefits beyond the access needed for vehicles.

"The sun sets perfectly at the wide end of the V," Mitchell explains. "In the evenings we wanted a space where light could pour in through the shutters and people could enjoy a bit of warmth in that courtyard. We wanted to be able to capture that warmth at the end of the day and keep it through the night."

Even though the new house was in a safer neighborhood, security remained a major consideration. The client insisted on having no windows on the ground floor, which made cross ventilation of spaces and access to natural light very difficult. Mitchell and his team decided to create a thick earth bag wall wrapping around the buildings' external facades. This type of wall has thermal qualities to compensate for limited ventilation. The walls and rooms facing the courtyard, meanwhile, are clad in thin wooden rod screens. In this way, light can filter all the way downstairs to the lower bedrooms.

The wood screens—made from leftover timber rods with their bark removed for use in veneers—let light in, and many of them are set in front of vibrant colors. "We love architects like Luis Barragán and others who really play with color. But we never make decisions around colors beforehand in the studio. Once you're on-site and standing in front of a wall or area, the colors come more naturally and in tune with the surrounding nature."

Gatheca loves the colors and is proud to have helped build some of the wood screens. He also learned how to work with plaster and took great pride in helping to build the house he would come to live in. The construction was expedited by twenty student volunteers from the United Kingdom working alongside community members, many of whom were learning skills for the first time. It's exactly that kind of training and local capacity building that Mitchell prioritizes in all his projects, but even he seemed surprised by where it led.

When the crew was packing soil into the earth bags, a local woman named Hellen Nyambura walked onto the construction site and told Mitchell she needed work. "Hellen approached me with this huge smile and incredible enthusiasm and asked for a job. I'd been turning guys away for weeks at that point, because we were full to the brim with laborers," Mitchell recalls. "I don't know why I said yes, but I did. I also challenged her, saying, 'You can come and you can work, but by the end of this project, you need to be the best mason on this site, and you need to be the best carpenter.'"

Mitchell didn't want or need Nyambura to be relegated to menial roles or cleaning or just moving things around the site; he wanted her to learn. And she had a lot to learn, having never been on a construction site.

design for good

← **Women position earth bags that will constitute a wall.**

Packing and laying the earth bags is tough work. The local soil, which has around 20 percent clay content, lent itself well to the packing process, but it is heavy. When stacked and staggered like bricks, the bags create thick walls that can absorb heat from the sun, helping regulate temperatures during the cooler nights. All told, over 4,000 bags needed to be packed and laid, each weighing more than fifty pounds.

"A week in, Hellen came up to me and said, 'I'm not enough on the site; you need to bring a bunch of my friends in as well.' I'm sure there was a bit of ploy there, but we ended up employing ten of her friends on the project," Mitchell explains. "They were incredible; they worked harder than the men, and they picked up skills quicker. By the end, Hellen was probably the most skilled earth bag person I knew, and now she can lay bricks and do all these incredible things that she didn't know before."

"We feel happy when we're working with men, as we are paid equally and thus feel we are equal," says Nyambura. "Never in my life would I have imagined this. I am used to tilling soil and washing people's clothes to earn a living, but when I found myself working with men on the earth bags—something that has never happened in Kenya—this made me feel very happy. We can't build our nation without either gender; we must work as one."

"Hellen taught us a lot that we didn't know about ourselves," Mitchell adds. "Now, on every project, we employ a minimum 50 percent women, and we've got some construction sites now that have 100 percent female workforces. All because of Hellen."

↑
Hellen Nyambura stands on her own land holding one of her children.

→
Hellen's House under construction, with its wood and corrugated metal roof and earth bag walls nearing completion.

design for good

The size and scale of the children's house necessitated using a crane to erect the large wood frames of the two buildings, which meant local laborers couldn't do that part of the work and missed out on some learning. In their visits back to the St. Jerome's Centre site in the couple of years since its completion, Mitchell and his team realized the gap in experience created by the crane was still being felt. People were saying they were grateful to know how to build an earth bag wall, but they didn't know how to apply lessons from this big structure to smaller ones, such as houses.

The dilemma, in part, led Orkidstudio to build a house for Nyambura and her children. This time, there was no crane and not even any drawings that would have required mathematics or engineering. It was all about teaching basic rules of thumb, according to Mitchell.

Nyambura was living at the time in a tiny two-room wooden house. "Everybody around there lived in pretty poor housing, but hers was the worst of the worst," Mitchell explains. "You could put your arms out and touch every wall if you stood in the center of each room. She was there with seven of the children. The eldest one had moved out."

Nyambura had her first child when she was eleven years old, and she went on to have eight children by two different and very abusive husbands. "Despite this, Hellen has such incredible positivity for the world, but she was clearly burdened. We decided that the best thing we could do for Hellen, in many ways to thank her, was to get her some land and build her a house," Mitchell continues. "But we didn't do it as charity; we offered it as a loan to her." Included in the loan were ten chickens and a small chicken coop. Nyambura and thirteen of her female friends did all the labor. It is a simple structure made of earth bag walls with a wood frame for the roof, which could be built without the need for a crane. The women got paid for their labor because it kept them from doing other work.

Previously, Nyambura's rent had cost her about 60 percent of her small monthly income. She almost never had enough to finish off the month. Mitchell came to realize that while Nyambura's may have been one of most egregious cases, she was not alone. In Kenya, it's very common for women in rural communities to be single with large numbers of dependents, and they typically don't own their land or their housing. In a very agricultural society, as in Kenya, if one doesn't have land for growing vegetables or keeping livestock, it's hard to earn a decent wage. All one can do is work for other people who own land.

Nyambura has been repaying Orkidstudio weekly for more than two years. She hasn't missed a week. As of this writing, she has scaled her chicken enterprise to about fifty to seventy chickens, and she is saving for a cow. She has more than tripled her monthly income, and in another three years' time, Nyambura will own her house outright.

"Hellen is truly one of the most remarkable people I've ever met," Mitchell says with sincerity. "She's responsible for the best aspects of our organization, in my opinion."

Shelter for the Soul

Although Orkidstudio still maintains a charitable arm, the group now operates primarily as a social enterprise. "I started to become quite jaded about charity and to feel that a lot of buildings, when gifted, can be taken for granted and risk becoming more of a burden on communities, rather than enhancing them," Mitchell explains. "I've always been really interested in entrepreneurship and business. I'm not one of these designers who has no idea about business."

More recently, Mitchell has been puzzling over how to build with communities more directly, rather than always with a nongovernmental organization as an intermediary. "When you work for an NGO, the NGO is your client, and they are representing the community. All you can really do is trust that the NGO is properly representing that community. But often NGOs necessarily have their own agendas, and the community's voice can be, or seem, lost. You can do as many community workshops as you like, but I still don't think they have total control."

To test its thinking, Orkidstudio is now piloting what might seem, at first glance, to be non-design work undertaken directly with communities. In Nakuru, for example, Orkidstudio is setting up dairy farms run by women and financed by the organization through bank loans. The women milk the cows, sell the milk, and make a profit. The organization takes a small cut of that profit as a shareholder, but the majority of the profit goes into a savings account, which then enables Orkidstudio to deliver housing for the women. Time and time again, Mitchell had encountered women who, like Nyambura, didn't own housing or land and were effectively trapped in a cycle in which they couldn't earn enough beyond their rent. Orkidstudio is determined to disrupt that reality.

It's clear that Mitchell and his colleagues care deeply about the people who inhabit their buildings and the many hands that help construct them. In our brief conversations, at times made difficult by language differences, both Nyambura and Gatheca repeatedly emphasized their sincere gratitude for Mitchell and Orkidstudio.

"I love this home they built us with us," Gatheca told me. "They changed our lives. One day, I hope to support Orkidstudio."

St. Jerome's Centre

Location: Nakuru, Kenya

Year completed: 2014

Built Area: 4,300 square feet

Cost (USD): $65,000

Client: St. Jerome's Centre
www.stjeromescentre.org.uk

Design: Orkidstudio
www.orkidstudio.org

Photography: Peter Dibdin
www.peterdibdin.com
Odysseus Mourtzouchos
www.odysseusm
-photography.com

A worker uses a trowel
to lay mortar during
the construction of the
St. Jerome Centre.

design
for
intention
Star
Apartments

↙
Aerial view of the Star
Apartments
(foreground), with the
Los Angeles skyline in
the background.

"I think of architectural design as language," a fast-talking Mike Alvidrez tells me, belying the profoundness of that statement. "That language says something to the user of whatever that space may be—whether it's a museum or concert hall, a university building or affordable housing."

A native of Los Angeles, Alvidrez is the longtime head of Skid Row Housing Trust. It's one of the most innovative organizations of its kind in the country, working under some of the most difficult of circumstances.

"Affordable housing of years past has always sent the message 'We don't really care about you very much, so that's why you're getting this element of design,' which is sort of anti-design in a way," Alvidrez continues. "We've all been through public buildings that are devoid of design. I don't mean 'public' for the general public, but public for poor people. Consistently horrible spaces, from housing to welfare offices.

"Back in the trust's early days, our focus was on preservation and affordability; it was just getting people off the street into housing," says Alvidrez. "We really didn't have an understanding of positive factors of homelessness nor the experiences that people went through. But by the mid- to late 1990s, we started to become much better educated as to the process that people have gone through, and we recognized we need to really ramp up the game."

Today, Alvidrez and Skid Row Housing Trust uniquely understand the detriments of uninspiring, institutional design, especially given their target population. Simply put, it says or reinforces to people already down on their luck that they don't matter. Although the trust's design sensibility has clearly evolved from its earliest days and projects, the organization has always taken great care to ensure its buildings don't replicate that institutional feel.

Chief among Skid Row Housing Trust's twenty-four buildings—all offering permanent supportive housing for formerly homeless individuals—are the Star Apartments. The six-story, 95,000-square-foot building includes 102 efficiency apartments and extensive public spaces and services for its residents.

↑
Street view of the
Star Apartments.

←
Ground-floor
reception area and
staircase.

design for good

For decades now, since the trust's founding in 1989, Alvidrez and his team have been at ground zero in the fight against homelessness. On the edges of Los Angeles's sleek downtown, with its world-class Walt Disney Concert Hall designed by Frank Gehry and its spectacular Cathedral of Our Lady of the Angels by Spanish architect Rafael Moneo, lies Skid Row. It represents the single largest and densest population of homeless people in the United States, with 6,000 people in the short span of fifty square city blocks.

During the 1980s, the City of Los Angeles lost and did not replace about 7,500 units of single-room occupancy (SRO) housing. The reasons varied, from change of use to demolition to fire, but it put pressure on the people who had relied on it as a last resort. They were often people struggling to live on fixed incomes or struggling with mental illness or addiction.

"The old demographic was white male alcoholics; that used to be the typical demographic of Skid Row," explains Alvidrez. "That changed, obviously, and it is much more racially diverse today. The reduction in the housing stock created a problem, and that's why the trust was created."

According to Alvidrez, though it hadn't yet figured out the answer, the trust asked, "How could we shape the space within our buildings to actually facilitate and be conducive to recovering from the side effects of homelessness?" Its best instinct was to incorporate social services in a way that didn't cause people to feel any stigma. That applied to medical, mental health, and addiction treatment services. Under the approach of Housing First, mentioned earlier in the discussion of The Cottages at Hickory Crossing, social services are not mandatory; they're all voluntary. They're also not the basis for housing but instead are the next step after housing.

The trust then had to convince providers to put their staff in its buildings, which was not the usual model. "It was very important for us to have services available to the residents on-site, so we designed office spaces that were well lit so that when we made the offer to our service partners, they would see that we really did design a space with them in mind," Alvidrez explains.

Beyond the services offices, the trust seeks to create options throughout its buildings that give people as many choices as possible related to outdoor and public spaces. The same applies to semiprivate spaces, where people who don't want to engage in activities with a lot of other people can keep to themselves.

"This is totally consistent with Housing First, where choice is so important," explains Alvidrez. "These are folks who basically have had very little choice in their own lives; they're often told where to go, what to do, how to do it, when to do it, and the right way to do it. And if you don't follow all those directions, you get sent back to the end of the line or dismissed entirely from that opportunity."

Alvidrez cites what he calls very forward-thinking leaders and administrators in the Los Angeles County Department of Health Services. "As in many other cities, they were seeing homeless folks with acute health needs cycling through their emergency rooms and their hospitals repeatedly, being discharged back to the street, not getting any better."

In 2013, this situation led the City of Los Angeles to create a division within the Department of Health Services called Housing for Health. "These crazy doctors think—and they have told us—that as doctors they can prescribe nothing better to improve the health outcomes of a homeless person with high health needs than supportive housing," says Alvidrez, himself in relative disbelief. He adds that the Housing for Health division expressly wanted to be on Skid Row and within the trust's new Star Apartments, so it leased a corner office space for its administrative offices.

→
Four stories of prefabricated modules are perched above the second-floor terrace and a ground-floor health clinic.

Shelter for the Soul

Open-air walkways
cross the interior
courtyard of the
Star Apartments.

The Star Apartments—comprising prefabricated components that were craned into place—is the work of Michael Maltzan Architecture, whose ties to Skid Row date back to its establishment as a firm.

Maltzan was born far from Skid Row, across the country on Long Island. He was raised in the routinely critiqued community of Levittown—a 1950s planned community widely regarded as the archetype for postwar suburbs across the country. Among the 50,000 people to first reside in Levittown, Maltzan surprises me with his positive view. "There was a lot of intention in putting those communities together. They've gotten a bad reputation over the years for lots of reasons—being fairly monochromatic and not very diverse—but they were built as places," Maltzan tells me.

Maltzan left Levittown for architecture school at the Rhode Island School of Design and graduate school at Harvard University, finally striking out on his own in Los Angeles in 1995. Among his first projects was one for a local nonprofit called Inner-City Arts. Speaking of the organization, Maltzan tells me, "They haven't been trying to create artists but instead to use art as a bridge between the young students' economic, social, and educational circumstances."

For Maltzan, however, it was a project that began not so much with a social mandate or a political ambition as with a real affinity for the arts. The work—ultimately leading to galleries and museums—took hold in Maltzan's office. Still, he explains, "I kept trying to look for a way to broaden the work and even to find places where it would seem less likely for architecture to exist."

"I took for granted, probably naïvely," Maltzan says, "that full engagement with the capabilities of architecture in culture and society was something that architects did. I was looking within my practice to build that capacity. The project started out more culturally and arts related, but I kept looking for opportunities to broaden the scope."

Seeing his firm's work for Inner-City Arts, Skid Row Housing Trust called and ultimately offered Maltzan a project called the Rainbow Apartments. The year was 2003. "I was ecstatic because I had really wanted to do housing. Housing was one of the building blocks of contemporary and modernist architecture and its relationship to society," Maltzan posits. "But no typical housing developer ever seemed to want to hire an architect like me. This project felt like it literally fell into my lap, and that's how we began."

By Maltzan's account, that first project, the Rainbow Apartments, was fraught with difficulties and complications. Construction was completed in 2006, when building costs were accelerating in the lead-up to the 2008 recession. As Maltzan's firm and Skid Row Housing Trust neared the end of the project, they were trying to find ways to cut things out of the building to recoup money.

"This is a joke, but it's not too far off that we were trying to figure out if we could use two screws in a door hinge as opposed to three screws. It was a very difficult process for everybody involved." Maltzan was dismayed but all the more determined. "When we got done with that project, I thought that the only way you could do these projects reasonably was to take the knowledge that you had just built up and bring it to bear on additional projects."

Skid Row Housing Trust is naturally incentivized to apply its learnings as well. It acts as both a nonprofit developer and a management company for two dozen buildings. So despite the difficulties encountered by all parties, Maltzan "went back to the trust and explained why my firm should do the next two buildings, to apply those learnings," he recounts. "That really was the beginning that led to this ongoing relationship, where we're now finishing our fourth building."

Looking back, Maltzan feels that each building has been a little bit out of each group's comfort level. With the Star Apartments, the fact that it was the first prefab building and was built over an existing building, not to mention all the city agency reviews, meant that there were a lot of moving parts to contend with.

Before the Star Apartments, prefabrication of multifamily developments was not allowed by the City of Los Angeles. Oddly, there wasn't even a path to getting it permitted, according to Maltzan. The Star Apartments were only the second prefabricated multihousing building in the city, with the first one in the 1960s, more than fifty years earlier.

The prefabricated components that make up the Star Apartments were all built in a factory outside Boise, Idaho. Although their construction was optimized for efficiency, the components had to be trucked almost 1,000 miles to Los Angeles. As a result, a significant percentage of the economic impact was in Idaho rather than Los Angeles. "One thing that's ironic about prefabrication is that while it is extremely efficient in terms of materials and energy used, most of these manufacturers are located far away from the place that eventually those units are placed," Maltzan explains.

"Based on our experience, I think sourcing locally is going to remain the job of the designer, or to make our concerns about local materials more prominent, more visible," says Maltzan. "I think leadership at the level of government needs to weigh in on this process to do that intelligently because they hold many more of the carrots in terms of how to incentivize projects to source more locally."

Since the project's completion, Maltzan has been working with both the county and city to look at the utility of prefabrication, especially regarding projects that deal with homelessness. One of his suggestions is to locate a prefabricator in Los Angeles County, closer to the sites that will be built using that technology.

"It's not so much that I would change the Star Apartments, but I think we know much more now; we'd be able to begin that project in a way where you could anticipate more how it was going to develop and where the issues were going to be." True to form, Maltzan adds, "I'd love to do another building that took on the same types of questions because I know we would be able to produce an even better building with this experience."

→
Each 300-square-foot unit has a kitchen and a bathroom.

design for good

Shelter for the Soul

One question I asked Alvidrez, which I asked virtually every person I interviewed, was "What is one thing that you'd like the residents or future residents to understand about this building?" His response startled me initially. "Nothing," he said, flatly. When I asked what he meant, he said, "Let me tell you a story."

A few years before the creation of the Star Apartments, Alvidrez and Maltzan had collaborated on another complex called the New Carver Apartments, also on Skid Row. The building's most iconic feature is a cylindrically shaped courtyard, which appears to be the swirling inside a tornado, frozen in time and space.

"We really wanted to bring as much light into the ground floor as possible," explains Alvidrez. "A guy we met with at the city's Community Redevelopment Agency, an architect himself, asked, 'Why do you care about that? Why don't you just close in that patio completely? Those people don't care about it.'"

Alvidrez goes on: "Aside from wanting to choke him with my bare hands, it was like he basically said, 'They won't understand it; they don't get it,'" with "they" referring to homeless people.

To Alvidrez, whether the residents consciously "get it" or not isn't as important as how they feel about themselves when they're in the spaces. It may not rise to the level of consciousness, and if it doesn't, he's perfectly okay with that. "If people get a feeling from a space, that is far more important than whether they can consciously understand what our intent may have been or what we hoped to see happen," he says. "For me, this is more about how people feel when they engage in those spaces. If they understand something beyond that, that's just icing on the cake."

People's experience of a place can also be very individualized, depending on their background and whatever trauma and unpleasantness they may have experienced in the past. "I just want them to sense that we took great care in designing the building for them," Alvidrez explains. "However that may translate to them individually, I'll leave it up to them.

"I know how it makes me feel when I go to that building," Alvidrez tells me of the Star Apartments. "I feel great. When I go to that second-floor deck, it has such a calming feeling. At the same time, there's kind of an inspiration and an excitement, so you've got these two things going on—both calming and stimulating. It's all totally visceral. But I still don't even experience it on a conscious level."

Speaking further about the elevated second-floor deck, Alvidrez adds, "I love being in that space. I love seeing people use the space. The residents clearly enjoy it, and I think that energizes and motivates us. If we can develop, in concert with our architects, spaces like that, which benefit the residents, it just tells me we're on the right track. We've got to keep doing it. We've got to keep refining it. We've got to keep thinking how we could best do that."

↑
The prefabricated
modules form a
courtyard connected
by open-air walkways.

Shelter for the Soul

When I asked Alvidrez and Maltzan who, specifically, informed their decisions on behalf of the residents, both pointed to a group of tenant managers who run the trust's buildings on a day-to-day basis. Those tenant managers live in the buildings and, in almost all cases, have gone from living on the street to being part of the organization. This type of intelligence gathering—not with ultimate tenants but with representative tenants—is crucial, both men tell me, since most residents aren't identified until late in the construction process.

The trust doesn't spend a lot of time formally surveying its residents. Alvidrez and Maltzan also don't see these people as subjects; they're relationships. The information they rely on is more anecdotal. "Very often, residents will speak to visitors," Alvidrez explains, "telling their own experiences. At the Star Apartments, what we hear them telling folks is that the overall benefit, aside from simply being off the street and in housing, is that second-floor deck. It creates that feeling for many of the residents where they can exhale for the first time in many years. They can feel safe. They can feel comfortable.

"It's funny; I think the thing that's been maybe the most surprising is how much resonance the project has had to people outside the social service and homeless communities," Maltzan explains. "That's one of the things that has been most exciting for me. As we were designing it, I didn't really think that it would become such a strong part of the conversation."

Though proud of his firm's work, Maltzan saves his highest praise for the trust. "They have continued to push the ball forward with each subsequent project. They have continued to be ambitious in terms of what these projects can represent and pragmatically do for these underserved communities, but also because of the responsibility these projects have to the city around them."

"If it can work on Skid Row, it can work anywhere," Alvidrez says emphatically. "The Star Apartments have become a model for truly aspirational thinking about how we should address homelessness and what people need in order to recover from it."

Star Apartments

Location: Los Angeles, California, United States

Year completed: 2014

Built Area: 95,000 square feet

Cost (USD): $19.3 million

Client: Skid Row Housing Trust, www.skidrow.org

Design: Michael Maltzan Architecture www.mmaltzan.com

Photography: Iwan Baan www.iwan.com

Shelter for the Soul

4.
Spaces That Enlighten

→
Mulan Primary School in Huaiji, Guangdong, China, by Rural Urban Framework and The Power of Love; completed in 2012.

Projects Profiled

Winston Churchill famously wrote, "We shape our buildings; thereafter they shape us." There is no institution more formative, in this regard, than the school building. This chapter presents three radically different spaces, all specifically designed to facilitate learning among at-risk communities.

Mulan Primary School in Guangdong Province, China, brings the best of design to a town that had poor public school facilities and a region relegated to standardized, government-sanctioned designs. In a time when rural communities in China are being pushed to urbanize, this building, designed by Rural Urban Framework, celebrates the local. It breaks from the monotonous design of traditional school buildings, sparking the imagination of students and serving as a gathering point for the community.

In Kalamazoo, Michigan, the Arcus Center for Social Justice Leadership serves as a hub for LGBTQ+ (lesbian, gay, bisexual, transsexual, queer/questioning) and other historically marginalized populations at Kalamazoo College, in its broader community, and throughout the world. While such centers are normally relegated to leftover spaces in student unions and other parts of campus, the Arcus Center was designed to publicly and proudly showcase the social justice work it facilitates. Even the construction of its distinctive cordwood masonry exterior was a community-building and learning exercise.

On to rural Rwanda, where Sharon Davis Design partnered with Women for Women International on the Women's Opportunity Center in Kayonza. Built with more than 500,000 bricks that were made and laid by the women themselves, the center is focused on empowerment. In the words of Virginia Woolf, it gives these women—many of whom have been victimized during the country's civil war—"a room of their own" to heal, learn, and grow together.

design
for
learning
Mulan
Primary
School

Architect Joshua Bolchover, a native of Manchester, England, grew up surrounded by the process of design. "My parents are architects, and they work from home, so my home was literally a living, working office when I was growing up. They were always dealing with problems associated with buildings," explains Bolchover. "I was fascinated by all the tools that surrounded me—scale rulers, Maylines, and all this kind of stuff.

"I always say that my biggest act of rebellion was actually becoming an architect, because it was something I swore I would not do," Bolchover continues. "My parents would always say, 'Whatever you do, do not become an architect.'" They had seen the social ambitions of architecture erode over the years. However, after exploring a career in medicine, Bolchover ultimately decided to pursue architecture, pledging to do it in a very different way from his parents, who had focused mostly on health-care architecture in Manchester.

Bolchover landed in Hong Kong after studying architecture and working in Cambridge, San Francisco, and London. The move to Hong Kong came when Bolchover was living in London, teaching, and doing multiple other things. "I was basically working three jobs, getting paid nothing, and thinking it was amazing," he explains. "Then we moved to Hong Kong, and I got a job working at the University of Hong Kong in a quite junior role. I remember this moment when they gave me the keys to my office and said, 'Okay, there you go.' I asked, 'Well, what do I have to do?'"

The implication to Bolchover, he tells me, was "'Just do what you do. Just decide what you do.' But they didn't even say that; they didn't give me any guidance whatsoever. It was a real moment of liberation, and I began wondering, 'Okay, what am I going to do here?'"

Bolchover soon met architect John Lin, whom we met in chapter 3. Lin was building a school in rural China and invited Bolchover to make the eight-hour car trip with him to visit it. As they talked and observed the transition from their urban lives in Hong Kong to the rural context where Lin was working, the two hatched the beginnings of their practice together, Rural Urban Framework, a research program of the University of Hong Kong.

As work on Lin's original school project concluded and under the auspices of Rural Urban Framework, Bolchover and Lin reached out to other nongovernmental organizations that they thought might need design assistance. That outreach connected them with a Hong Kong–based NGO called The Power of Love, which for nearly two decades now has been building schools across rural China. Purely by coincidence, it also had a tie to the University of Hong Kong.

The NGO was created by Ivy Lam, a Hong Kong native who was educated in Canada and returned to become an administrator in the Department of Medicine at the university. Grateful for the opportunity she'd had to study, and aware of the limited educational opportunities for most children in rural China, Lam established the NGO in 1998. Since that time, The Power of Love has sponsored more than one hundred schools in fifteen provinces across China where educational opportunities are limited.

Virtually every one of the schools that The Power of Love supported was designed and built to the specifications of the local government or education authority—predominantly concrete buildings with flat roofs and single-loaded corridors. "It's seldom that we can have a specific design for the schools," Lam explains, "in part because the cost can be higher."

Lam routinely shared photos of the schools and students she worked with through her NGO while at her day job at the University of Hong Kong. A colleague and neurologist, Ho Shu Leong, was intrigued: "These are people, young kids, in extremely rural areas. Their parents are usually subsistence farmers. And I could see what a difference better-designed schools would mean to them."

Ho's late mother was a schoolteacher, and he had the idea of sponsoring a school in her honor. Ho, who describes himself as very careful with his charitable donations, implicitly trusted Lam because of her work in the Department of Medicine, where she managed a multimillion-dollar budget. Ho decided to join Lam and a group of people she had organized on a trip to one of the school sites in mainland China.

Lam, Ho, and thirty students and their parents made the eight-hour bus trip from Hong Kong to the northwestern part of China's Guangdong Province. As the group was just getting settled at the school site late in the afternoon, the sky darkened and a huge thunderstorm swept through the area. Both the group and the local students they had traveled to meet took refuge from the sudden, torrential rain in the existing school building, which had only four classrooms, a leaky roof, and no electricity.

→
One of six classrooms in the new Mulan Primary School building.

"I could see that the students from the village knew exactly where the roof would leak, so they moved their dilapidated wooden tables and chairs to try to avoid getting wet," Ho recalls. "Meanwhile, I sensed the fear in all the kids and parents from Hong Kong." When the rain subsided, the students and parents from Hong Kong quietly trudged back through the muddy road to their bus while the local students went home to their families, some walking an hour or two to where they lived.

When Lam got her group back to their hotel in a nearby town, as well as dried off and warmed up, she sat the students in a circle and asked them to write about their experience. Ho recalls, "These kids wrote down really, quite surprisingly, very sensible stuff—talking about what they learned from this episode. The students wrote about how they could see the difference in the reaction to the torrential rain and lightning and thunder between them and the local kids. You could see how fortunate these kids from Hong Kong suddenly felt to study in a safe environment."

Following their return to Hong Kong, Ho told Lam he had been thinking about the beautiful area they had been in but also the leaky school building they had seen. He wanted to make something better. Through the University of Hong Kong, Ho had also learned of the work that Bolchover and Lin were embarking on with Rural Urban Framework. He wondered what they could create with Lam's organization if they weren't wedded to the design stipulated by the local government.

"The Power of Love had sat down with the local students and said, 'Draw your ideal school.' All the kids drew their ideal school, and they all turned out to be basically the same," Bolchover explains. "They were all the same concrete buildings. That's all they knew. Their reference points were clearly demarcated that this is what a school should look like."

Moments like this remind me of a quote long attributed to carmaker Henry Ford: "If I had asked people what they wanted, they would have said faster horses." It is ultimately the challenge of designers to help people imagine a better future and to expect more.

With Ho's encouragement, Bolchover and Lin decided they didn't want this to look like every other school; they wanted to give the students something all their own, uniquely attuned to enhancing their learning experiences. "We knew we could create very different spaces and offer a variety of learning environments," Bolchover explains. "In our design, each classroom has a slightly different geometry, and each has its own identity."

That special identity gets carried through into other spaces in the building, such as the small courtyards and the larger outdoor spaces. "I think these differentiated learning environments and social spaces are very much missing within the typical institutional makeup of schools in China," Bolchover says. "It's limiting the social interaction that occurs among the kids themselves and also within the villages."

The group knew the approval of the local government would be difficult, but essential, to get. At the outset, both the school and the government wanted to demolish the existing school building to make way for the new one. According to Lam, it was Bolchover and Ho who advocated for keeping and renovating the old building, which dated back to the 1950s. It afforded additional space, and it could be improved with the addition.

So Bolchover and Lin focused their design on the relationship between the existing and new buildings, with the goal of adding another five classrooms and a library. The new building is adjacent to the old building and connected by a series of steps, which double as outdoor space for classes or for village events.

Community use of the space was important to everyone involved, and it is a hallmark of Rural Urban Framework projects. "In China, the village is the one space where people can democratically elect a leader, the village chief," Bolchover explains. "In our projects, you'll see that we're always trying to see that the school, or whatever building it is, is not a kind of walled, gated compound but is very much open and a space for the village to access and gather."

Ho was especially interested in sustainable design. "I was committed to designing it with local materials and local labor that could leverage some of the strengths that village has to offer," he explains. "Sustainability is also one of the top concerns recognized by the government of China. The second biggest concern is sustaining the local community, the people who will look after it. That's always my belief as well, and one of my principles: local people looking after local interests."

Although the village near the school was impoverished, Ho tells me, "it's not as if they're lacking materials there. They had all the local materials to be able to build anything. It would be such a waste to have imported expensive materials from outside the area, which would have also added to the cost."

Bolchover and Lin often visit materials markets where they're working to explore unintuitive options for building. "In this case, we found a unique silver tile, which we were quite excited about because it creates this weird mirage effect as you move it," Bolchover explains. "It's slightly reflective but also blurred, so it creates this cool visual effect as the children move around. We were interested in using that silver tile as a way to create a kind of optical effect within the courtyard space.

"We started very much thinking, 'Okay, we've got only this limited palette.' The structure has to be concrete, post and beam construction. We have to use brick infill. So we were thinking, 'How can we make the most of those limitations in order to create interesting spaces?'" Bolchover continues: "Of course, the budget's limited. Yet even if we had excess money and budget, I don't think we'd go for more extravagant materials or methods. It's this interesting play to really push the limitations and see what we can get out of them."

Of the more than one hundred schools that Lam has sponsored, she calls this one "unforgettable." Lam explains: "The school is a model in so many respects and one we're very proud of. It's very difficult to build a nontraditional school in China, because we have to go through a lot to clear the government restrictions. That involves a great deal of work with the local authorities and also the workers; when they build something different, there is a lot of uncertainty and a lot of things to learn. This particular school took about twice as much time as our regular schools, but it was worth it."

design for good

Spaces That Enlighten

"Schools and buildings are one thing. But as an educator," Ho tells me, "I know that the biggest leverage, by far, for children to escape the cycle of poverty is education itself. I strongly believe that. Ivy and her organization have provided this opportunity to get kids educated. It's the biggest investment anybody can make, to try to improve the lives of these kids and their parents." Ho continues: "Eventually, who knows, one of these kids might turn out to be a super farmer, learning all these new things and able to improve the way they do things, the way they plant their rice. Or maybe much more."

When Ho returned to the school for the opening ceremony, he noticed that a plaque had been hung to recognize where every dollar had come from, including Ho's contribution. Ho recalls, "It was the exact sum, down to the last dollar. It was a very matter-of-fact type of statement."

Although he knows his mother would have been proud, Ho wasn't impressed with having his name on the list; he was moved by the names that followed it. "The names were of the parents of the students, some donating just a very small amount of money, but that wasn't the point," Ho continues. "These people could hardly afford to dress their kids, let alone donate to a school building. These local farmers donated in whatever way they could to the school, and the school recognized that. I knew that investment meant that they would take care of it. They would not only take care of the school structure; they would also take care of the surrounding environment."

During a family visit, Bolchover brought his father to see one of their other projects, also a school, elsewhere in rural China. "My father loved it, because he could really see what village life was like in China and that what we were doing was impacting people in a really basic way."

Bolchover's parents are socialists at heart. "That's one of the reasons why they settled in the United Kingdom, where my dad is from, in the late seventies; that was the moment when the National Health Service had been set up. It was a very optimistic period for the country as a kind of social welfare state was being established. Architects played a role in the creation of that welfare state, but it has been completely diminished over the past thirty years, and they've witnessed that.

"For my parents to see some of those socialist instincts still present in contemporary society—and to have Rural Urban Framework reclaim some of that space that has been overlooked quite significantly in architectural practice, at least over the past ten, twenty years—I think that's something that my parents feel reassured and hopeful about."

Mulan Primary School

Location: Huaiji, Guangdong, China	
Year completed: 2012	
Built Area: 5,500 square feet	
Cost (USD): $90,000	
Client: The Power of Love	
Design: Rural Urban Framework, www.rufwork.org	
Photography: Courtesy of Rural Urban Framework	

design for good

↑
Students play in the
courtyard of the school.

Spaces That Enlighten

design for
solidarity
Arcus Center
for Social
Justice
Leadership

"When people first visit, I always spend lot of time talking about our building before I talk about what we do," Mia Henry tells me. "I want them to know that the space they're in was intentionally designed for the work that we plan to do together."

Henry is speaking of the Arcus Center for Social Justice Leadership, a breathtakingly beautiful building on the Kalamazoo College campus in Kalamazoo, Michigan. In our conversation and my visit to the building, I was instantly reminded of how sharply it contrasts with the spaces that most social justice organizations occupy on college campuses across the country.

All too often, student groups and even academic departments that focus on racial and ethnic diversity, LGBTQ+ issues, and women's studies—some of the many areas expressly related to social justice— seem to be relegated to the basements of campus buildings or leftover spaces. Rarely do these spaces reflect the change that these groups work so hard to see in the world. Some do exactly the opposite, providing a daily reminder of their occupants' "otherness" or subordinated status. Fewer still appear to be designed for their unique users, much less with them.

With a dedicated center, programming under way, and an endowment to support the work, Kalamazoo College was in a unique position to make social justice leadership a centerpiece of its mission. Although driven by the college, this work was catalyzed by the generosity and support of an alum, Jon Stryker, who brought to the table not just the resources to make it possible but also a deep commitment to both social justice and design.

A native of Kalamazoo, Stryker is the founder of the Arcus Foundation, dedicated to the idea that people can live in harmony with one another and the natural world. He's also trained as an architect. Speaking of the collective ambition for the project, Stryker tells me, "We wanted to impress on people how important social justice leadership is and to make it strongly embedded in the campus culture, as well as have a visible presence in the Kalamazoo culture."

design for good

Stryker had the ultimate ally in Eileen Wilson-Oyelaran, who was serving as president of Kalamazoo College at the time. Born in Los Angeles and raised in Southern California, Wilson-Oyelaran had spent time in East and West Africa. She was the first woman and the first African American to hold the post of president at the college.

Before the concept of the building itself, the idea of the Arcus Center was born as Stryker, Wilson-Oyelaran, and the center's director at the time considered the needs of the college and of the world. Initially, it was to be a social justice center. Their collective research revealed several models for social justice centers in institutions of higher education, particularly law schools. Most of them focused on global human rights, LGBTQ+ issues, community service learning, or civic engagement—all of which were already well-developed facets of Kalamazoo College.

Wilson-Oyelaran and her team sought input from the generation of activists they intended to serve. "It became very clear that there was going to be a huge generational change in social justice leadership," she explains. "Many activists who are my age, who came up in the 1960s, had training in activism but not the other kinds of training that we ended up finding we had to do: raising money, communicating, and, now, utilizing social media and building global connections."

When the decision was made to forgo renovation of an existing build-ing on the site and build a totally new facility, the Arcus Center became Wilson-Oyelaran's first major capital project. "We had done some work on the campus, including the renovation of our student center, but I am someone who by nature has not been given the gift of spatial intelligence," she jokes. "In other words, I don't know squat about building anything."

Before her tenure in Kalamazoo, Wilson-Oyelaran had been involved with a building project for a YWCA in North Carolina. "One of the major questions we asked the architects in the case of the YWCA was about the involvement of women and people of color in the project," Wilson-Oyelaran recalls. About three years after that YWCA project was completed, the lead architect came to Wilson-Oyelaran and said, "Because of that question, we established an internship program for architects of color."

"I learned a lot from that process," Wilson-Oyelaran says, "so when I got to Kalamazoo College and we were doing the student center, I said, 'We're an institution that needs to value diversity and inclusion in the buildings we build.' I would say to all the companies involved, 'Tell me what your staff looks like.'" She brought that same conviction to the Arcus Center building project. "We also made a real effort to ensure that the subcontractors were people of color or had women involved in the process," Wilson-Oyelaran explains. "We wanted every piece of the work to reflect the values that the Arcus Center embodies. That was one thing that was very important to me."

The college explored a variety of architects, ultimately engaging Jeanne Gang and her Chicago-based firm, Studio Gang. Gang was born in the small Illinois town of Belvidere, where her father was a road and bridge engineer and her mother was a community organizer, or "activator," as Gang called her. The family was of modest means, but they recognized that others had far less.

"Part of my upbringing, especially through my mom's example, was learning how to serve others. Although I probably never imagined exactly what kind of buildings I would design, the service aspect of my upbringing is very much part of who I am," Gang tells me. "It's not just me, though. All the people I've surrounded myself with in my practice are similarly engaged and like-minded."

The road trips Gang and her family took when she was growing up opened her eyes to the built and natural world. At home, she would build tree houses, forts, and, in the winter months, elaborate igloos. She would find or make a huge pile of snow and then take hot water that her parents boiled for her and carve out very organic spaces within the pile. It taught her the limits of what would stand up or collapse while also giving her an appreciation of form making.

The interior provides
a range of work
spaces for individuals
and groups

Gang completed both her undergraduate and graduate degrees in architecture and went on to work at the office of OMA, the firm of celebrated architect Rem Koolhaas. She then struck out on her own, establishing Studio Gang in 1997. One of her firm's best-known projects is a Chicago skyscraper called Aqua Tower. At nearly 900 feet tall, it is the third-tallest building in the world designed by a woman.

As Gang and her firm set about trying to identify models or precedents for social justice centers, they found very few in the traditional sense. What they uncovered instead was the importance of spaces such as church basements and kitchen tables. There were some community gathering spaces in other cultures, such as deep, stepped wells in India, where people gather as they collect water or wash their clothes. But on the whole, Gang and the college realized that they were conceiving of a new type of building.

"There is a concept among the Yoruba, my husband's ethnic group in Nigeria, about what happens in the place where roads meet. That point is called orita," Wilson-Oyelaran shared with the group. "As we talked about the Arcus Center building as a place that would bring the campus and the town and nature all together, that was very exciting."

Wilson-Oyelaran's suggestion of the building as a crossroads resonated with Gang and her firm, giving form to the plan. Gang loved the ambition of the college to make the building not just another campus building but a truly public space in which to gather. She was also drawn to the LGBTQ+ advocacy work that is part of the Arcus Center's mission. "We collectively had a real desire to make the center's work visible to the outside world—even in spite of the fact that there can be dangers in doing that. There are people who hate the LGBTQ+ community, so there are risks," Gang acknowledges. "But we all felt it was important to make this work really visible, really proud."

Internally, the building is designed to facilitate conversation, from group gatherings to more intimate one-on-one conversations. Two unique elements of the building were expressly designed with dialogue in mind: a kitchen to cook and share food in and a hearth. Neither, of course, is standard or even permitted in public spaces of most buildings, but Gang thought they were worth fighting for. "Both are such primary human needs," she reminds me. "Gatherings help people open up and talk."

While some colleges and building donors might have erred on the side of a more traditional design or elected to forgo elements such as the kitchen and hearth, Gang had an ally in Stryker, the project's design-conscious funder. In the early 1960s, at the age of two, Stryker moved with his family into an architect-designed home that his parents had commissioned in Kalamazoo. It was a modernist house with flat roofs and a koi pond, both influenced by their architect's studies in Japan. To get to the front door, visitors had to cross a bridge over the koi pond.

Stryker recalls other influential buildings in Kalamazoo, including an art institute downtown designed by Skidmore, Owings & Merrill in a very contemporary international style. "That really had an influence on my aesthetics," Stryker recalls. "I went to art camp there and was very fortunate to have that as an amenity. It was new at the time, and I remember it well because it was the first time I had ever been in a building that was air conditioned."

Stryker studied biology as an undergraduate student at Kalamazoo College and had distinct memories of the Arcus Center site. The building that was there originally was the college president's house, and then it was renovated as an academic center focused on the business aspects of the community and the college. Stryker, who went to architecture school at the University of California, Berkeley, worked for an architectural firm in Kalamazoo that designed an addition to the back of the former building.

Before pursuing a totally new building, the college's original plan had been to renovate the existing house on the site one more time for the Arcus Center. Stryker, however, wasn't convinced it would be adequate for the scale of their ambitions: "I thought the center needed a building that really honored the work, celebrated what people were doing there, and made it a destination on the campus and for the community."

Stryker is clear that the vision originated with the college. "They really own this work. We kind of planted the seed, but it grew within the college. They designed social justice leadership as a program that infiltrates the entire campus and all the programs, and that's really what appealed to me," Stryker continues. "It's not often that you get an opportunity to invest in a school and change its trajectory as we've been able to do.

"I'm a believer in architecture, and I would say that buildings are important to the work that happens inside them," Stryker explains. "They influence the way people interact and engage with each other."

↑
The main interior space is bright and open, accentuated by the curved walls.

Mia Henry, executive director of the Arcus Center, grew up in the South and counts Alabama as home, but she spent fifteen years in Chicago pursuing an array of work. She started her career as a high school teacher and then took to nonprofits to get youth involved with civic engagement and politics.

Henry founded the Chicago Freedom School, based on the 1964 Freedom Schools established during Freedom Summer in Mississippi, which was a black voter registration campaign led by prominent civil rights groups. In a similar vein, the Chicago Freedom School works with young people aged fourteen to twenty-one to help them develop or join campaigns to advance social justice issues.

During her fifteen years in Chicago, Henry considered herself a big fan and admirer of the city's architecture, occasionally going on architectural tours throughout the city. She and friends also worked to save a couple of buildings from demolition. Still, Henry explains, "I always feel like what's missing from a lot of the architectural gems that we revere, including where I was in Chicago, is that you kind of look at them from afar and you admire them, but you don't really use them. You don't really see them as part of your life."

Thus, the Arcus Center's mandate to be a public building for the community really resonates with Henry: "It's important that people in the community see the building as a place that belongs to them."

Community members are able to reserve the building free of charge. Henry explains: "It aligns with our social justice goals of making the college itself less elitist and more accessible to people in the community." The center's values are part of the building's reservation form, so individuals and groups seeking to use the space are reminded of those principles.

Spaces That Enlighten

design for good

↙
**Elevation view showing
the depth of the
cordwood masonry walls.**

Another defining feature of the Arcus Center building is its unique cordwood masonry, which is effectively walls made of short logs placed widthwise in the wall, with one end exposed. The logs are set in and spaced apart by thick mortar, as in a brick wall. On their routine drives from Chicago to Kalamazoo, Gang and her team stumbled across a hundred-year-old barn in Michigan. "It was just one of those things where we were like, 'How in the heck did they do that? This barn is lasting forever,'" Gang recalls. "We wondered if we could try to revive that and bring that building technique into the twenty-first century."

Studio Gang learned that the technique has virtually no carbon emissions, as the cordwood effectively sequesters carbon and the wood is entirely untreated. It also enables use of almost 100 percent of the tree trunk with virtually no waste, as the diameter of each piece can vary. The challenge was that the wood needs approximately a year to dry, so the college had to commit to the facade quite early in the design process.

Since the technique was new to everyone involved, Studio Gang organized a workshop and full-scale mock-up on the site. The gathering included community members, people from the college, and the contractors. "When the professional masons on the job site saw what they had created together, they said, 'Wow, we can do that too,' Gang recalls. "They ended up doing it so fast. It was unbelievable. So there was some help during the real construction, but most of the community building was done in this mock-up that allowed us to envision what the building was going to be.

"Our theory was to get people involved with what they were going to have before it actually was built," Gang explains. "But it really goes to show that our practice is deeply into making. Modeling at full scale helps us discover things. Then you can start to work with the design given those rules that you discovered."

The resulting walls range in depth from twelve to eighteen inches. The building technique is similar to that for creating a brick wall in that the cordwood masonry wall is self-supporting, but there is also an air gap and then an insulated interior wall. The cordwood acts as extra insulation, another advantage in Michigan's climate.

Gang's team also did a lot of testing with the color and composition of the mortar to determine the placement and resulting density of the wood. They wanted to leave only the smallest possible joints or spaces between the wood, to achieve more of a blend or fabric feel and avoid a spotted appearance. As light and shadow pour over the facade, the cordwood really comes to life.

Buildings can have a variety of emotional effects on people, despite an architect's stated aims. Gang insists, especially in this case, that she's far less concerned about people's experience with the building itself and much more interested in their encounters with other people in the space. "A lot of times, as architects, we think, 'How do you want people to feel when they walk in?' Like feel elated, or feel free, or whatever. The point of this building, for me, is to try to get beyond the individual."

Gang wonders, "How can we as architects help people to form relationships with each other? How do we do that?" She continues: "My hope would be that visitors to the Arcus Center would engage with someone who they maybe wouldn't necessarily talk to otherwise, or have a deeper conversation or more meaningful dialogue than expected. Hopefully, the building will help that to happen—that it will create a feeling of openness to others and make you want to be with others."

"I really feel like the college and center have embraced my values," Stryker notes. "But, of course, a lot of my values developed there in the first place. The Arcus Center building in particular has been really affirming and meaningful for me. I hesitate to use the word 'church,' but we knew we wanted a solemn kind of space that was still fun and celebratory."

Although Wilson-Oyelaran is now retired, the building's impact remains profound for her as well. She remembers the grand opening being particularly poignant because so many people who had put so much effort into the building were there together—the architects, builders, students, staff, faculty, and community members. "The next morning, I went into the building by myself, at about seven in the morning," Wilson-Oyelaran recalls, "and it was the most incredible spiritual experience. There's something about that building that offers a kind of energy. I don't have the technical terms, so I can only talk about what I felt. When it is not filled with people, and you are able to be enveloped in the space, it can feel quite spiritual. Or at least it did for me."

The highest praise comes from one of the people who work in the building day in and day out: "I'm very fortunate to be able to work in a beautiful space with smart people doing important work," Henry shares. "There are not a lot of people who can say any one of those three things, much less all three."

She sums it up: "The building has truly become a beacon for the work that we do and for the community."

Arcus Center for Social Justice Leadership

Location: Kalamazoo, Michigan, United States

Year completed: 2014

Built Area: 10,000 square feet

Cost (USD): $5 million

Client: Kalamazoo College
www.kzoo.edu

Design: Studio Gang
www.studiogang.com

Photography: Iwan Baan
www.iwan.com

↑
**Evening view of the
Arcus Center.**

Spaces That Enlighten

design for empowerment
Women's Opportunity Center

↙
Gardens and farming
plots are terraced
down the sloped site.

Each day, upward of one hundred women flock to a community center that, for many, is like a second home. That was always the goal. Not only was the place designed for and with these women, but many of them literally helped build it with their own hands. The center is the vision and a program of Women for Women International, a global NGO started in 1993. The organization is uniquely focused on women in countries affected by war and conflict, such as Rwanda.

The natural beauty of the Women's Opportunity Center site in Kayonza, a rural community approximately one hour's drive from Rwanda's capital city, Kigali, belies the ongoing struggle many women there continue to face. Countless women were raped and victimized during the country's horrific civil war in 1994. Their personal healing, and the healing of the country, continues.

"Although there is more activity and development there, Kayonza is still primarily agrarian. It's surrounded by a lot of people who farm for their livelihood, whether on formal farms or squatter farms," explains Karen Sherman, who played a key role in initiating and leading the project during her long tenure with Women for Women International.

"What we really thought the center could be was a gathering space for women, not only for training but also for their economic activity," Sherman continues. "We hoped it would be something that was contributing not only to the women but to the entire community."

Sherman selected the site, on behalf of Women for Women, and remembers being struck by the beauty of it and the views on her first visit. There were some banana trees and other vegetation but nothing that was being cultivated. In this site, as in the women she worked with, Sherman saw huge potential.

Sherman, who is American, has dedicated her career to international development. Much of that work has related to women, including the decade she spent as chief operating officer and executive director for global programs and, ultimately, Africa regional director for Women for Women International. The organization provides educational, financial, and interpersonal support to women who are survivors of war, poverty, and injustice. Although Sherman left the organization in 2013, it's clear from our conversations that the Women's Opportunity Center is a particular point of pride for her.

design for good

←
Steel roof structures above the administration buildings and classroom pavilions serve as water catchments.

As she transitioned to focus on Rwanda and the center, Sherman and her three children relocated from the United States to Rwanda. "To have my kids there with me was an amazing experience, as a mom who has been doing international development for a long time, but also for my kids to have that opportunity," Sherman explains. She put together a business plan for the center and oversaw its construction.

Beyond some small home renovation projects, Sherman hadn't ever really thought about design or architecture as a way of connecting with people. She had always approached her work more from a global development standpoint. The center, as she reflects on it, just happened to be a unique project where those two things came together. "We wanted it to be a safe space for women, something dedicated to what we call their 'learning, renewal, and progress,'" Sherman explains. "For women who had already benefited from the organization's work before the center, they could come back there for advanced training. We saw it as a chance for women to refresh their skills and to learn new skills that would help them to earn an income."

One of Sherman's key and early partners in undertaking the project was Sharon Davis, principal of New York–based Sharon Davis Design. "Sharon is just such an open, inquisitive person. She really wanted to understand what we would do with the center, how it would operate, and what was the intentionality of the center," Sherman explains.

"Sharon, her team, and our people spent many, many, many conversations talking about the center's use and culture and about the women and what it would mean to them. We talked about what it might look like but even more about how we wanted it to feel," Sherman continues. "I don't know how other projects work, in terms of the marriage of development and architecture, but I just thought Sharon's whole approach was really unique and thoughtful."

Davis's path to the Women's Opportunity Center and to architecture generally was anything but a straight line. Davis intended to become a painter, but when she grew disillusioned with the commercial art world soon after college, she rerouted to business school. She entered an investment bank training program, and for two years she pursued her master's degree in business administration at night at New York University, followed by a decade in the investment business. "During that time, I didn't produce anything; I think I was more of an appreciator and an admirer of the arts," Davis says.

In her forties, with four children at home and her youngest just three years old, Davis decided to get back to her love of the visual and go to architecture school. She graduated on the brink of the 2008 recession, knowing she didn't want to apprentice in a large firm, as most graduates do. Shortly thereafter, she got a phone call out of the blue from Women for Women International.

"One of my friends did PR consulting for nonprofits, and she was in a board meeting with Women for Women when they found out that they had secured the land. One of the board members in the meeting said, 'I'll provide the funds to build the school,'" Davis explains. "Then they all kind of looked at each other and said, 'Well, we need a woman architect.' None of them knew one. So my friend recommended me." It would become Davis's first project.

The donor and the founder of Women for Women met with Davis, who was very candid about the fact that she didn't have any experience. "I talked about what I cared about, which was sustainability. I explained that I also didn't know anything about working overseas or working in developing countries," Davis explains. "The donor was really interested in having the women make the bricks, which would bring multiple levels of sustainability to the project. We just kind of clicked over that and she said, 'All right, I'm going with you.' It was a very serendipitous moment."

In addition to having limited design experience, Davis had been to Africa only twice, as a tourist, and never to Rwanda. At the time, however, there were only a few architects in the entire country of Rwanda. Any nervousness was eased by the warm welcome she received from the Women for Women staff in Rwanda and, soon after, from the women for whom the center was ultimately intended.

"I had direct access to the women, which I now know is very unusual. It never occurred to me that access to the actual users of a space was so rare," Davis explains. "I had translators, so I could ask them any questions, and the things they were saying were translated for me. I felt like we had this very intimate connection almost immediately."

The women told Davis about their daily lives and, in many cases, what they had endured during and following the country's civil war. Those stories were incredibly hard to hear, but Davis empathized with the women, creating a unique and strong bond.

As she stood overlooking the site, Davis was humbled by what she saw in front of her. "It was absolutely gorgeous. We were standing on this road, on top of this hill, looking out over this green valley, and it was so beautiful. My first thought was, 'How could anyone put a building here? It's too beautiful.'" Knowing that the buildings were inevitable, Davis immediately started thinking about how low-rise structures with curved rooflines might mimic the rolling hills beyond, foreshadowing the design to come.

At another point on that first trip, Davis was sitting in on a class that was focused on health and social welfare, including an array of topics such as human rights, women's rights, and birth control. The women shared stories about their lives, their children, and their husbands. Most of the women had never held money, let alone had their own money.

As Davis and the team were driving back from the class, she was struck by all the women walking down the road with yellow jerry cans, going to get water. "I remember thinking, 'How can women who are taking care of children and have to cook with a wood fire every day be spending hours collecting water and also be expected to have jobs? This is crazy,'" Davis continues. From that moment forward, water became central to the project.

Initially, Davis and her team did a solar study to see how light and shadow would impact the site. Their process led to a sort of ovoid shape. In short order, the roof design started to double as a rainwater collector—an idea that stuck and became a hallmark of the project.

But the catchment system also came with some surprises. It worked so well that Women for Women had to put in a third cistern. Despite having previously had to walk significant distances to get water, however, some of the women came to take it for granted, as is human nature. It became part of their new normal.

→
A class gathers outside one of the classroom pavilions.

↘
A group gathers in one of the pavilions; the bricks were made and laid by the women themselves.

Spaces That Enlighten

Both the brickmaking and brickwork represent another hallmark of the center. Women for Women had already started a brickmaking cooperative as one of the vocational skills it offered, stemming from a small grant that predated the center. The challenge was to scale it up.

"The actual training was much harder than we thought, of course," Davis concedes. She and her team went through a long process of determining whether the primary building material should be earth blocks or fired bricks and determining the sustainability and the strength of each. All told, the women produced every one of an astounding 500,000 fired bricks used to construct the seventeen pavilion classroom structures and other parts of the center.

Another challenge was cultural. "When I first arrived in Kayonza, there was a lot of building going on, but I didn't see a single woman on any site," Davis recalls. Davis and her on-site project architect, Bruce Engel, pledged to get women directly engaged in the construction.

"The architects would often talk about 'brick by brick,' but I always looked at what we were doing as woman by woman," Sherman explains. "These women were literally rebuilding their lives, and these bricks became a manifestation of that."

Floor tiles were made by Congolese women in another Women for Women program. "What a statement about women's productivity—having the floor tiles and brick walls all made by women," Sherman exclaims. "Architecture and buildings like this center are a means; they're not ends unto themselves. Our means related very much to the mission of Women for Women and what we were trying to accomplish in our longer-term goals of women's economic empowerment and income generation. There was a reason to do this, but not just to build buildings."

←
Street view of the shops and market, where women at the center can sell goods and food.

→
Each classroom pavilion is circular to facilitate discussion.

Shortly after the center was completed, Sherman and her family left Rwanda, and Women for Women went through some structural changes. Sherman recalls, "My vision of a fully utilized center didn't really manifest, at least immediately. I think Sharon felt the same way." She continues: "Literally, the worst thing you can think of is to spend a lot of time and a lot of money, and then nothing happens. From a development standpoint, there are many defunct projects funded by aid and other development organizations."

Sherman and Davis's understandable disappointment was short-lived, thankfully. "When I was at the center on my last trip," Sherman explains, "I saw a high level of activity there. There's a beautiful store, there's a coffee place. Women are making peanut butter and yogurt. That was what I really wanted to see at the center—that kind of action, women learning things, women making things, women building community."

Sherman was succeeded as Africa regional director by a Rwandan woman named Antoinette Uwimana. Though long familiar with the organization's work, Uwimana joined Women for Women in 2013, just after the launch of the center.

Uwimana was born and raised in the Democratic Republic of the Congo to Rwandan parents who were refugees. She started her career as a teacher and then served as a deputy governor for the eastern part of Rwanda during the reconstruction that followed the 1994 civil war. Since that time, and for most of her adult life, Uwimana has focused on development and women.

On her first day at the Women's Opportunity Center, which she had only heard about previously, Uwimana was blown away by what she saw. "It's such a beautiful place. It's something that attracts a lot of curiosity but also admiration," she explains. "Seeing such an eco-friendly design is just amazing—from the collection of water to the composting toilets and more. Everyone is so proud of it.

"Every woman who is using the center is generating something," Uwimana continues. "Women are selling their products, but they're also learning about leadership and business skills. And they're making money for themselves and their families.

"The center is busy almost every day. There is a market for food and products made by the women. On a daily basis, we also have groups of women coming, doing their activities, like the handicraft traditional artwork. We have the large restaurant and a very nice roadside café, which is really working," Uwimana continues. "And we have many visitors, including some tourists now and people coming to stay at night.

"For many of the women, this is more than a women's center. They feel at home here. It's their place. It's very, very meaningful," Uwimana explains. "They have their own spaces, their own corners, their rooms where they sit or work, where they keep their tools. It's really very meaningful for them."

The project became the foundation of Davis's practice, which continues in Rwanda and now extends to other countries, including Nepal. "We became involved in this particular project largely by happenstance, really," Davis says, "but so much of it has informed our work going forward, in terms of using local materials, using found objects, hiring women, hiring unskilled labor, and then teaching them a skill that they can then go on and be employed to do.

"It has become an important part of our identity—working inexpensively, coming up with creative solutions, and still creating spaces that people feel good in and feel that they are appreciated," Davis continues. "I just want each person to know that someone cared about what they were making for them."

When I asked Davis what she had thought she would end up doing when she first left finance to go to architecture school, she told me, "I thought I was going to be doing residential apartment renovations in New York City, and I thought I'd be totally happy. After projects like this, I really can't imagine doing work like that."

As for Sherman, in her new role as president of the Akilah Institute for Women, a nonprofit education program based in Kigali, she continues to be influenced by the Women's Opportunity Center and the experience she gained in creating it. While it was Sherman's first major capital project, the Akilah Institute has had some discussions about building a campus in the future.

"If I were ever to undertake any kind of capital project again in the future, I would be incredibly mindful about how it would be used, how people would interact with the space—all in a different way from how I would have before the Women's Opportunity Center," Sherman explains. "I also would ask a lot of other questions that I wasn't able to articulate while working on the center. I know a lot more now—I guess the good, the bad, the ugly. But I also have a greater appreciation for beauty."

Women's Opportunity Center

Location: Kayonza, Rwanda

Year completed: 2013

Built Area: 24,000 square feet

Cost (USD): $1 million

Client: Women for Women International
www.womenforwomen.org

Design: Sharon Davis Design
www.sharondavisdesign.com

Photography:
Elizabeth Felicella
www.elizabethfelicella.com

↑
A cluster of classroom
pavilions are aglow as
night falls.

5.
Places for Civic Life

→
Bait Ur Rouf Mosque in Dhaka, Bangladesh, by Marina Tabassum Architects; completed in 2012.

Projects Profiled

Our communal instinct to gather—to play, to protest, and everything in between—is primal. The three places profiled in this chapter are crucial hubs for culture and community. They vary in scale and purpose, but are all focused on bringing people together.

The Atlanta BeltLine, miles of reclaimed railroad corridors and trails around Atlanta, Georgia, is years in the making and still very much in its early stages. It is an exercise in audacious thinking and an example of repurposing old infrastructure to breathe new life and connectedness into disenfranchised communities. With only a portion completed, it is already reenergizing the city of Atlanta while catalyzing new development.

The Bait Ur Rouf Mosque in Dhaka, Bangladesh, is both a sanctuary for religious practice and a vital gathering place for an underresourced community. Designed by architect Marina Tabassum in honor of her late mother, the mosque is known as the "House of the Compassionate." Forgoing many of the symbols traditionally associated with mosques, the building is elegant in its design and construction and is very clearly a labor of love.

Finally, returning to the United States, we have the Lakeside Senior Apartments—the work of David Baker Architects and a partner specifically focused on developing affordable housing. Nestled in a dense neighborhood just blocks from a large lake in urban Oakland, the apartments help the seniors—many of whom have experienced homelessness—reconnect with civic life.

design for
reclamation
Atlanta
BeltLine

↙
**Aerial view of a
completed section
of the BeltLine.**

A colorful, intricate map that architect Ryan Gravel drew in graduate school now hangs in Cooper Hewitt, Smithsonian Design Museum in New York. That's hardly the norm for any graduate thesis, and perhaps it was the last thing that the understated Gravel could have ever imagined.

Gravel's thesis project, or what is now known as the Atlanta BeltLine, is a twenty-two-mile loop encircling the city of Atlanta, Georgia. Threaded through a once busy industrial railroad corridor, the Belt-Line is envisioned to be like a string of pearls, with nodes of parks, public art, housing, and transit—all connected by smooth paved trails.

The entirety of the BeltLine lies within the confines of the city of Atlanta; it is only three miles out from downtown in any direction. To date, only portions of it have been completed. Although the vision is grand, the seeds of this extraordinary project are much more humble.

Gravel was born on Barksdale Air Force Base in Shreveport, Louisiana. At age two, he moved with his family to Metro Atlanta, which he counts as home. "I was a quintessential American suburban kid from the seventies and eighties," says the blue-eyed, once blond-haired, Gravel, whose hair is now a stark white.

In 1991, while an undergraduate student at the Georgia Institute of Technology, Gravel left the familiarity of Atlanta for a study abroad program in Paris, along with a couple dozen classmates. "After a month of living there, I had lost about fifteen pounds," Gravel recalls. "I was in the best shape of my life."

For Gravel, the role of the city in his health and well-being became immediately evident. Having grown up in the suburbs of Atlanta, he thought it inconceivable that he would walk everywhere, much less barely get in a car for an entire year.

On his walks through the cobblestone streets and bustling sidewalks of Paris, Gravel became obsessed with the role of infrastructure—roads, alleys, transit, and the like. He began to see infrastructure as "not just the foundation for our economy but also the foundation for our social life and culture," he recounts. It struck him that infrastructure shapes the way we live, whereas in architecture school, individual buildings were presented as paramount.

Paris's signature expressions of infrastructure are its grand boulevards, which were plowed through the medieval city in the mid-1800s. They came with a great social benefit, drying up the wet, dank streets and dramatically improving public health in the process. They provided paved surfaces for carts, wagons, and later cars and buses.

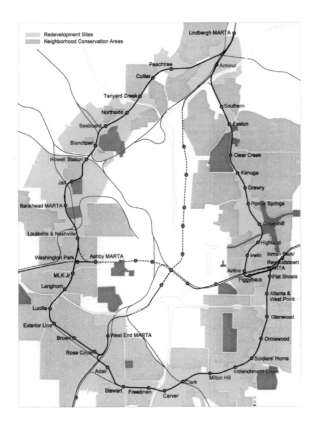

They also provided water and sewer and public spaces as well as trees and, eventually, electric street lighting and subways. For Gravel, learning, seeing, and experiencing such a radically different way of life was a revelation.

Returning to suburban Atlanta's car culture in 1995 proved to be a rude awakening for Gravel. He settled into his first architecture job, which necessitated driving across Atlanta's perimeter highway to and from the office. The task at hand was even more soul crushing: designing office parks. "You sort of mow down the hillside of trees and replace it with rows of single-story office buildings alternating with surface parking lots," he recounts. "I realized that I was part of the problem and not part of the solution."

It was around that time that Gravel started to reconnect with a childhood obsession, railroads—themselves a form of infrastructure. Atlanta was once a major junction for the railroad, and the sprawling city grew around it. On a whim, Gravel started studying and visiting the old railroad corridor that wrapped around Atlanta.

As freight trucking surpassed rail shipping, the rail corridors saw less and less use. Moreover, the rails became dividing lines between communities, literally giving rise to "the other side of the tracks." While the city lost industry and population in the 1970s and 1980s, throughout Gravel's youth, Atlanta started growing again in the 1990s—not with industry but with commercial and residential developments attracting people back into the city. Still, with a current population of 450,000, Atlanta itself accounts for only one-tenth of the 4.5 million regional population.

In 2001, Gravel and a few coworkers mailed copies of the map he had stitched together as a graduate student to every elected leader they could think of. They wanted to generate some support for the idea and simply thought that's what elected leaders are for. Thankfully, one of those recipients agreed: the map landed on the desk of an Atlanta city council member named Cathy Woolard. "I went into my office, and there was a big manila envelope on my desk," she recalls. "Inside, there was a typed page of every elected official in the state of Georgia—from Senator Max Cleland in the upper left corner to lowly me in the bottom right corner." On the second page was the map. "It's like folklore in Atlanta."

An Air Force brat herself, Woolard had spent part of her childhood in Georgia and the rest in an array of far-flung places. Among her experiences were four and a half years spent in Europe that, she recalls, "really opened my eyes to what transit-oriented and walkable cities can do for a person's spirit."

Gravel's surprise delivery couldn't have arrived at a more opportune time for Woolard. She represented a district in Northeast Atlanta that was starting to experience gentrification, with land prices approaching $1 million per acre. Smack-dab in the middle of her district was part of that abandoned rail corridor, viewed by many as blight, overrun, and a magnet for illicit activities.

In her city council capacity, Woolard came to serve on and chair the city's transportation committee. Discussions usually centered on airport access and included very little about infrastructure such as the railroad corridor, much less the very real transit needs of her community and constituents. To her great dismay, Woolard discovered that the city didn't even have a transportation planner, much less a transportation plan. The committee simply responded to proposals as they arose.

Woolard realized instantly that the map Gravel had sent her addressed two key problems. One was the question of where to put transit in her district, and the other was how to start building a coherent transportation plan for the city more broadly. It also gave clues on how to address the density and development issues putting pressure on her district.

Woolard promptly summoned Gravel and some of his coworkers to her office. What she said surprised them: "I don't know how to do this; it's a very complicated project. We'll figure it out together, and I'll really dedicate myself to this."

It marked the beginning of an almost twenty-year working relationship between Woolard and Gravel, which is changing the face of Atlanta.

To build support for the BeltLine, Woolard and Gravel launched a grassroots campaign. Their first public presentation came at a small town hall meeting in the basement of a church in Woolard's district. Gravel arrived with his tattered thesis map and a carousel packed with slides. The duo patiently waited for their turn at the end of the meeting and then shared their vision. They planted a seed. Of those early days, Woolard remembers more questions than anything, some as simple, blunt, and incredulous as "What in the world are you talking about?" But the questions quickly gave way to palpable curiosity and excitement.

That fall, Woolard was elected city council president, taking the BeltLine case and cause citywide. Woolard, her staff, and a handful of volunteers, including Gravel, attended countless community meetings over the next two and a half years. "We created this movement—this truly, honest to God, grassroots movement of people who wanted something different," Gravel explains with no small amount of disbelief. "People fell in love with the vision for their future that was better than what they were seeing and better than what the city was offering them."

Soon, Gravel and Woolard were inundated with interest and requests. The Centers for Disease Control and Prevention (CDC) called out of the blue, saying it thought the project had interesting or positive public health implications. This had never occurred to the pair. In 2004, the Trust for Public Land got involved, swelling the project from 700 to over 1,400 acres of parkland. In 2007, the Georgia Tech Center for Quality Growth and Regional Development teamed up with Emory University's Rollins School of Public Health and the CDC for a health impact assessment.

"The idea, not only then but still to this day, continues to grow," Gravel explains. "People have a sense of ownership and authorship of this project, and it allows them to add their own piece to it."

By 2009, mayoral candidates in Atlanta couldn't be viable without supporting the project and having some plan to show how they were going to build the BeltLine better and faster than the next. "It was a really powerful political position to be in," Gravel acknowledges.

Today, the completed stretches of the Atlanta BeltLine are frequented by thousands of people each day—walking, running, and biking—especially before and after work hours. "We have free yoga in the park where there's a big field, and hundreds of people come to do yoga on Tuesday evenings," Woolard describes. "For people who live along or near the BeltLine, I think it really has transformed their ability to have healthy lifestyles."

A lasting memory for Woolard came while she was biking on a stretch of the BeltLine one afternoon around midday. Riding back from a meeting, she saw two different men, both in motorized wheelchairs. "One of them had a service dog with him, and both of them were going hell for broke down the BeltLine," she recalls. "It was a beautiful day, their hair was blowing back, the dog was just running full-on with his tongue hanging out."

Her excitement evident, Woolard continues, "I thought, 'God! This is exactly what the project was meant to be!' If these two guys can live on the BeltLine, they've already got two and a half miles of completely accessible pathway where they can get to a grocery store, parks to see concerts and other activities, restaurants without getting into a car or trying to navigate Atlanta's horrendous sidewalk situation."

A huge part of the BeltLine's success, Woolard believes, will be its permanence. "My firm belief is that if you can put in a permanent transit infrastructure, then the private investment will surely come."

The public investment is estimated to be upward of $450 million, but it is projected to leverage $10–$20 billion in economic development. Other figures include 45,000 jobs to construct the full project and adjacent property plus 30,000 permanent jobs. More than 5,000 units of housing are planned, with approximately 500 realized as of this writing.

Because of its name and reuse of old rail lines, the Atlanta BeltLine is often compared with the celebrated High Line, an elevated public park in New York City. Stretching for a mile and a half along Manhattan's West Side, this section of elevated rail was itself inspired by a similar project in Paris called the Promenade plantée, completed in the early 1990s. The High Line's cost was more than $300 million, but for one-tenth the land area of the BeltLine. Still, the billions of dollars in private investment sparked by the High Line provide potent evidence for the potential of the BeltLine.

For those who still think $450 million is too much money for a city like Atlanta to invest, Gravel is quick to point out that the city currently spends billions of dollars on highway infrastructure. "We're not asking those highways to consider their impact on the communities in the city or out of the city. We're not expecting them to address affordability or equity. We're not asking them to do anything other than serve cars." Although one might counter that they do enable people to get to their jobs.

Gravel goes on, "If we asked our infrastructure to do more than just one thing, I think we would make a lot of different decisions. And I think the world that we created would be much more sustainable and healthy and equitable."

→
People move
along a walkway
on the BeltLine.

Places for Civic Life

Woolard's best advice to others embarking on public projects of any scale is to "start community engagement early, and be sincerely open to listening to what people have to say."

Similar to the High Line and other successful projects, Atlanta is now experiencing a rapid increase in property values along the BeltLine. Both Woolard and Gravel attribute that partially to the popularity of the project but also to the comeback in the real estate market.

"People are concerned about property values increasing, but I don't get the sense that people don't want the project," Woolard explains. "There's still enough buy-in all over the city for people to say, 'Yeah, we want this project. We just want to make sure it doesn't screw us up,'" referring to gentrification and other forces. Speaking of that loyalty and trust, Woolard explains, "I really believe that civic engagement just won it all."

Looking back, Woolard says, "We were probably naïve enough. We always believed it would happen. We simply didn't know enough to think it wouldn't happen."

When pressed on whether the BeltLine can be seen as a model for other cities' efforts, such as the well-publicized Los Angeles River Ecosystem Restoration Project now under way, Gravel is quick to point out that it's not about a particular type of infrastructure. "What I've learned is that it isn't so much about having some old railroad or degraded waterway," he explains. "The key thing is just a way of thinking about infrastructure; it's about asking our invest- ments in infrastructure to do more than just one thing."

Atlanta BeltLine

Location: Atlanta, Georgia, United States

Year completed: Ongoing

Area: 22 miles

Cost (USD): $450 million

Client: Atlanta BeltLine Partnership, www.beltline.org

Partners: Atlanta BeltLine, Inc. Atlanta BeltLine Partnership, www.beltline.org City of Atlanta, www .atlantaga.gov, Invest Atlanta www.investatlanta.com

Design: Perkins+Will www.perkinswill.com

Photography: Christopher Martin www.christophertmartin.com FlyWorx www.flyworx.co Ryan Gravel www.ryangravel.com

↑
The Historic Fourth
Ward Skatepark along
the Eastside Trail is
Atlanta's first public
skate park.

design
for
ritual
Bait Ur Rouf Mosque

"Buildings, for me, are living beings. They breathe. They have a soul of their own."

So says architect Marina Tabassum, the unlikely designer of the Bait Ur Rouf Mosque on the outskirts of Dhaka, the capital city of Bangladesh. Tabassum was born and raised there, in what she describes as a war-torn nation.

"Design has mattered since I learned to think. But I also grew up with the experience of seeing people struggle to meet the basic needs of life," Tabassum explains. "In many ways, it came as a realization that architecture has a much larger goal that goes beyond architecture. That's why, through my design, I'm always trying to optimize the resources available to build a better living for others." It's fitting, then, that the Bait Ur Rouf Mosque is also described as the "House of the Compassionate."

Tabassum's family owned land in the northern end of Dhaka, one of the fastest-growing cities in the world. Within the past two decades, areas that used to be farmland had turned into settlements for lower- to middle-income families, but community facilities were not keeping pace, particularly since these areas were not included within the main city administration or planning. The community needed a place to pray together. Bangladesh represents the fourth-largest Muslim population in the world, with more than 90 percent of the country practicing Islam.

In 2002, Tabassum's mother passed away unexpectedly from a severe allergic reaction. "That was one of the lowest points in my life. I was struggling quite badly to cope with the tragedy," Tabassum explains. Her grandmother, who had suddenly lost her firstborn child, decided to donate a portion of her land for a mosque, giving Tabassum the responsibility of designing and building it. "She asked me to design it because I am an architect and she could also sense my suffering. The project eventually became a process of healing for both of us."

Despite the inspiration, the benefactor, and the architect all being women, in Bangladesh there is not a strong culture of women going to mosques to pray. Most mosques do not have space for women to pray, as has been the case since the arrival of Islam in Bengal in the fifteenth century. "But I remember, as a child, going to the neighborhood mosque early in the morning to learn to recite the Quran," Tabassum says. "My memories of the cool terrazzo floor, the fresh morning breeze, the light of dawn with the sound of recitation created an atmosphere of tranquility and spirituality that has remained with me through my life."

Tabassum was exposed to an array of religions while studying at an American missionary school called Holy Cross Girls' High School in Dhaka. "It was a multi-religious environment; I had friends who were from many different faiths. We celebrated all the religious festivities, like Eid at the end of Ramadan, Christmas, and Puja," she explains. "Religion, to me, is about respecting the diversity that exists among us and enhancing the values that are humane."

→
The stairway to the
upper floor is made of
perforated sheet metal
to allow air and light to
pass through.

Places for Civic Life

design for good

Places for Civic Life

Within just a few years of her mother's passing, Tabassum's grand-mother became ill. Tabassum decided to hold a groundbreaking cere-mony even though they had raised only enough money for the foundation. The event took place in September 2006, under a jackfruit tree next to the mosque site. Tabassum invited her family and the community to join in a short prayer, after which she and her grand-mother announced the donation of land for a mosque. Her grandmother passed away shortly thereafter, in late 2006. It would take another six years for Tabassum to raise the money needed to complete the project. As funds became available, she made incremental progress, but in total the project took twelve years to finish.

From the very beginning of her design process, Tabassum made a conscious decision to forgo symbolism. Instead, she wanted to focus on what is essential in the religion. "I researched the first mosque in Islam to find out why it came into being. It was conceived as a place of congre-gation. Muslims gathered in brotherhood, all as equal, in complete submission to one omnipresent God," Tabassum says. "There was no symbol, no ritual, only intense devotion and spirituality that connected man to the divine."

Although commonplace in most mosques, symbols such as domes were introduced only in later times for functional reasons, such as spanning large spaces. Minarets were used for the purpose of calling people to prayer. To Tabassum, "what matters is the quality of space where one stands to pray, not the symbols. Because prayer is a form of meditation and of internalization.

"There is no prescription in Islam about the elements of a mosque," Tabassum continues. "There are a few obligatory requirements for congregational prayers, such as a fountain to wash hands before prayer, but as long as those are satisfied, any place on Earth that is clean can be used for prayer."

The Bait Ur Rouf Mosque was the first mosque that Tabassum designed, but she has always been interested in public projects. In 1997, only the second year of Tabassum's career, she and Kashef Chowdhury, her partner in a firm called URBANA, won a national competition to design the Museum of Independence in Dhaka. The project took many years to complete because of changes in the government, but it finally opened in 2015. The entirely underground museum is part of a sixty-seven-acre complex at the site of a historic speech declaring the struggle for independence. It was the same site where Pakistani forces surrendered in 1971.

"For all my public projects, I believe it's important to grow a sense of ownership among the user group. Without that, it's impossible to ensure the healthy life and use of a building," Tabassum explains. "I always have people's feelings in mind while designing. I design emotion and journey through space. That's why projects like the Museum of Independence and the Bait Ur Rouf Mosque touch people so much: because they were designed to connect with people."

←
Men kneel on the terrazzo floor in prayer.

→
Apart from being the spiritual center for the local community, the mosque also serves as a community center.

Tabassum's uncle, Zulfiqur Hyder, who acts as general secretary of the mosque committee, has been involved in various capacities since the mosque's inception. Hyder also is originally from Dhaka. He served in the army, retired with the rank of colonel, and now works for a heavy-duty construction company that builds roads, bridges, and other large infrastructure.

Since it was his family's land, Hyder watched the area around the mosque develop for years. "A mosque was a long demand for the local people because there wasn't one in the vicinity. Many people had to walk a mile or more to the next closest mosque to say their prayers. One was very much wanted in this particular area," Hyder explains.

"If you see other mosques in our country, they are all quite similar and symmetrical. There's always a big dome at the top. There are usually one, two, three, or more minarets," Hyder continues. "These are distinguishing features that tell people that these buildings are mosques.

"In our country, mosques are typically made, but this mosque is designed, and Marina took quite some time giving a lot of thought on how to construct it. I very much like the design of the mosque, especially the lighting and the air circulation," Hyder says. "These are important environmentally friendly features."

Hyder also likes that the main gathering space of the mosque is wide open, without any center columns, accommodating as many as 700 people. He describes the hall as cool and beautifully lit. "People really appreciate that their hall is quite suited to their prayers," he adds.

Hyder explains that, as Tabassum intended, the mosque is also being used when there is no prayer. "People who are poor or don't have any other place to go to school are being taught there. The teachings relate not only to religious life but also to the general education of the kids."

The budget, Tabassum points out, was modest. "Since all the funds were raised from local people, we had to use only materials that are locally available and easy to construct with local labor. As such, except for the prayer hall, which is raised on eight peripheral columns in concrete, the rest of the construction is a load-bearing brick structure." Bangladesh has a rich culture of brick architecture. Two-thirds of the land that the country sits on is a delta, providing the perfect soil type to make bricks.

As in Tabassum's childhood mosque, the floor of the main hall is terrazzo, in this case made from stone dust collected from local factories. The floor really comes to life when light streams in through small holes in the roof. Those holes are covered with glass, so not open air but sunlight pierces and moves across the space. Tabassum adds, "The most important element in the design is daylight, and that is for free."

Traditionally, as Hyder noted, mosques are constructed but not designed. Tabassum explains: "It is usually a matter of following what is an accepted norm for a mosque—copying the elements, shapes, and sizes, at times in correct proportions, but most of the time crudely. In a city like Dhaka, one can find numerous examples of poorly constructed mosques. The rich legacy of mosque building that was initiated with the advent of Islam during the Sultanate period is lost entirely.

"Among the few mosques designed, the number by architects who happen to be women is even rarer," Tabassum concedes, while eschewing the title "woman architect." "I love and enjoy every aspect of being a woman. But when it comes to my work, I am a professional. There's no gender attributed to that.

"I do not think men have greater capacity to innovate than women when it comes to pure intellect. I never think I'm doing anything more special than what my male colleagues are pursuing in their professional careers." And while it's clear that the Bait Ur Rouf Mosque is one of the first in the world to be designed by a woman, if not the first, Tabassum contends, "If I'm to be applauded, it should be based on the merit of my work and not on my being a woman."

The mosque has drawn acclaim the world over, although the initial response from some, including the community, was as Tabassum predicted: "Where is the dome? Where is the minaret?" But, she observes, "Once the space was built and they started praying, the satisfaction of a quality prayer was enough to make them understand that those symbols are not necessary."

Places for Civic Life

↑
A man faces the mihrab,
a semicircular niche in
the wall of a mosque.

→
Daylight pours into the
mihrab, which indicates
the qibla or direction of
the Kaaba in Mecca.

design for good

Places for Civic Life

"My intention was that this be used as a space for the community to gather for different occasions, be it a wedding or a funeral. It's quite a large space to accommodate life's numerous moments of joy and grief. To use it only five times a day during prayer, and then to leave it empty for the rest of each day, would be a waste," Tabassum adds. In addition to the mosque serving as a day school for children learning the Quran, Tabassum is trying to initiate an hour daily for women to come and learn basic aspects of Islam.

Hyder, meanwhile, visits the mosque at least once per week, for Friday prayer, and sometimes more frequently. With recognitions such as the prestigious Aga Khan Award for Architecture, the mosque has attracted visitors from all over the country and beyond.

Initially, Hyder's response to whether the mosque made him proud surprised me. "No, I'm not proud," he stated firmly, and then paused. "My mother did not donate this land for a prize or anything like that. She donated this land so that people would come and pray here. She gave this land exclusively for that. For that, we are proud."

Bait Ur Rouf Mosque

Location: Dhaka, Bangladesh

Year completed: 2012

Built Area: 8,100 square feet

Cost (USD): $150,000

Client: Sufia Khatun

Design:
Marina Tabassum Architects
www.mtarchitekts.com

Photography:
Hassan Saifuddin Chandan /
Marina Tabassum Architects
www.mtarchitekts.com
Rajesh Vora / Aga Khan Trust
for Culture, www.akdn.org

↑
The column-free prayer hall
is raised on eight peripheral
columns, in addition to four
light courts.

Lakeside
Senior
Apartments

Aerial view of the
Lakeside Senior
Apartments
showing the
proximity to Lake
Merritt, with
downtown Oakland
beyond.

Bruce Baugh, age sixty-five, is not likely what you picture when you hear the label "senior citizen." A retired trucker with over two and a half decades on the road, the muscular Baugh looks as if he just walked out of a gym, tank top and all. He lives in the Lakeside Senior Apartments, just a couple of miles from my own home in Oakland, California.

Baugh confides in me that he doesn't work out or even walk around nearby Lake Merritt. "I'm retired!" he proudly proclaims. As we belly up to his kitchen table, Baugh tells me about his life on the road. He worked long hours and was never able to save as much as he would have liked. In his final five years of driving, he leased his own rig, only to see his expenses grow as he incurred costs that an employer normally would have covered. Spending weeks on the road, he hadn't maintained a home in years. But that meant he had no home to return to when his truck lease fell through.

Baugh slept on couches of friends and family thereafter, but he also spent many nights sleeping in his car. A church helped him find housing in a shelter, and a friend ultimately turned him on to the Lakeside Senior Apartments. These experiences make him all the more grateful for the one-bedroom apartment that he now calls home.

"I love it. I just love it, especially after being homeless for a while," Baugh explains. "Once you don't have something, and if you're fortunate enough to come out of that, you realize how lucky you are." One of its first residents, Baugh is especially glad to have scored a top-floor corner apartment. He proudly points out its steady cross breeze on an unusually hot afternoon.

With a stick of incense burning in the living room, a boxing match muted on the television set, and talk radio streaming from a small boom box in the kitchen, Baugh's apartment is clearly his. It's also meticulously clean, with the bed perfectly made and everything in its place.

When I ask what he likes most about living at Lakeside, Baugh doesn't miss a beat: "The neighbors, and not just the people on my floor but in the whole building; I'm the neighborhood watch guy." In fact, Baugh was elected to the important post by his neighbors without his knowledge, and he has embraced the role.

Baugh says hi to everyone we pass on our walk around the building, including the residents, janitor, and office staff. He loves the social interaction but also values the comfort and privacy of his apartment.

The need for affordable housing throughout the tech-rich San Francisco Bay Area is well documented. Rents in Oakland have skyrocketed since 2011, at a pace reportedly unmatched by any other city. Housing is generally considered affordable if it constitutes 30 percent or less of a tenant's income, including utilities. According to 2000 U.S. Census data, now dated by seventeen years, Oakland's median home income was $29,278, meaning rental costs would have needed to be roughly $750 per month, a fraction of what they are today. As of December 2016, the average rent for a one-bedroom apartment in Oakland was $2,754—nearly four times that 2000 census figure.

Seniors, many of whom rely on a fixed income, are particularly challenged to find affordable housing. The Social Security Administration's Supplemental Security Income program provides basic support, but the supply of senior housing units remains extremely limited. Most facilities have years-long waiting lists.

While the need has only increased, Oakland has experienced a dramatic decline in new construction of affordable housing with California governor Jerry Brown's 2010 move to defund redevelopment agencies. Statewide, $2 billion was cut; in Oakland—where Brown previously served as mayor—that amounted to $25 million annually.

The Lakeside Senior Apartments project was developed by Satellite Affordable Housing Associates (SAHA) for seniors just like Baugh. The organization's director, Susan Friedland, is the daughter of a foreign service officer who was frequently on the move. She recalls how

↖
**A resident looks out
from the fifth-floor
community space
toward the lake.**

↑
**A senior resident
walks along the
building toward
Lake Merritt.**

constant travel, mostly in Europe, influenced her as a kid: "That experience really framed my vision for walkable, mixed-use communities."

Early on, Friedman struggled to reconcile her love for these vibrant communities with the lives of the disenfranchised in their shadows. "Even as a child, I was deeply moved and concerned about homelessness and people suffering from lack of housing," Friedland recalls. Her twin interests in the built environment and social justice led to a liberal arts degree from Brown University, with the chance to take classes at a top design school, the Rhode Island School of Design, just a stone's throw away, and then to the University of California, Berkeley, for her graduate work in city planning.

Friedland's work over the past twenty-five years has centered on affordable housing. She spent a decade of that time at a community-based nonprofit in Brooklyn called Fifth Avenue Committee, rehabbing old buildings into housing mixed with new construction. After she cut her teeth in the hustle and bustle of New York, Friedland relocated to the West Coast in 2004, to the nonprofit Affordable Housing Associates, which, following a merger, would become SAHA.

The merger brought together two leading nonprofit housing developers, with one focused generally on affordable housing and the other on senior housing. SAHA's properties house more than 4,000 residents throughout Northern California.

Friedland is part policy wonk, part finance geek, with the heart of a social worker. She speaks as passionately about real estate transactions as she does about the residents served by affordable housing. Friedland summarizes her organization's mission as "creating great neighborhoods and housing opportunities for people who have otherwise been left out of the market."

When Friedland and SAHA were embarking on a below-market senior housing community for the rapidly gentrifying city of Oakland, they turned to a reliable source, tapping Bay Area architect David Baker, principal of David Baker Architects (DBA). Home making is part of Baker's DNA; he is well-known for his firm's multifamily housing, ranging from heavily subsidized to market rate.

Baker is the son of a migrant farmworker who went on to become an artist and self-trained architect. Back in the 1940s, his father read the autobiography of Frank Lloyd Wright and decided to build a solar house for his family in Michigan. Still, despite his exposure to design, building, and housing, Baker maintains, "I had no inkling, while I was in school, that I would do affordable housing."

Baker's firm was no stranger to Friedland or her organization. And Friedland, for her part, was no stranger to design. On multiple occasions, SAHA had enlisted top Bay Area firms for its wide-ranging projects—from a small cohousing community in a town north of San Francisco to a seventy-unit senior housing community in another part of Oakland. "I think by the time we worked on this project with DBA, we knew what we were looking for," Friedland confides.

↑
Lush landscaping surrounds the courtyard.

In 2009, a handful of years into Friedland's tenure, groundwork was laid for what are now the Lakeside Senior Apartments. The site, adjacent to Oakland's Chinatown, comprises three parcels of land pieced together by the Oakland Housing Authority. The most significant of those parcels was previously a surface parking lot for some adjacent senior housing.

In U.S. cities, few things are better protected by cities and more prized by communities than parking. The architects and client had their work cut out for them, since the site couldn't accommodate the requisite number of parking spaces per unit. They commissioned a parking study but also pulled crucial data on car ownership from SAHA's portfolio of properties. In a family of four in other SAHA properties, the average ownership is 1.1 cars, compared with 2.8 cars per family of four in the United States as a whole; in a senior household of other SAHA properties, the average ownership is less than half that. All told, the ninety-two-unit Lakeside Senior Apartments has twenty-three parking spaces designated for residents and another thirty-six spots reserved for an adjacent senior housing facility whose parking lot was displaced by the building.

A significant percentage of Lakeside's residents are monolingual Chinese. Like Baugh, many residents have experienced chronic homelessness. Selection for the units was based on a lottery run by the organization in conjunction with the Oakland Housing Authority. For those ninety-two prized spots, literally thousands of applications were received.

Since such lotteries take place after the design is largely completed, Baker explains, "We really rely on our clients," referring to SAHA. "They have very specific ideas as to the needs of the future residents. These are active seniors. We really design for what we think people will like."

Baker adds that he himself qualifies by age to live there (the minimum age is fifty-five), so he knows a thing or two about the demographic. "People tend to stay in affordable housing a really long time. It's nice, and the rent doesn't go up, so people are able to age in place."

Residents such as Baugh find ample privacy and comfort in their apartments, which are connected by corridors flooded with daylight. Small sitting areas and nooks are sprinkled throughout the building along with larger public spaces, including a protected interior courtyard, the popular rooftop community room—with its sweeping views of Lake Merritt and downtown Oakland beyond—and a yoga studio, among others. The residents care for and cultivate a series of small gardens in the courtyard and on the roof deck, growing vegetables in many of them.

↑
Street view of the
building with its
predominantly white
exterior standing out
against the beautiful
blue East Bay sky.

←
The building is topped
by a fifth-floor suite
of community spaces,
including garden plots
for residents, a
community room and
kitchen, decks, and a
wellness studio.

Dividing the building into two volumes, the architects created a transition between the nearby high-rise and smaller residential buildings in the neighborhood. The top floor of the building closest to Lake Merritt is stepped back in response to neighbors' concerns. And care was given to protect the light and views enjoyed by those in the adjacent buildings.

The architects used an array of materials—from wood to steel—to make the building visually dynamic. Large panels of color help differentiate the facades. With vertical lines drawing the eye upward, the exterior is unapologetically modern, yet it feels at home in a neighborhood of eclectic buildings.

Three separate entrances welcome residents. Inside, the space is clean and contemporary, without the sterile look and feeling of many senior facilities. Baker and his firm are known for sweating the details, and the building has plenty of them, between the materials and framed views. Internally, the main courtyard, for example, is visible from the street through an elegant corten steel and glass fence, but it maintains a sense of security for the residents. Adjacent to the property is a thriving neighborhood, with ready access to walking and biking paths around Lake Merritt.

→
The ground-floor community room opens into the courtyard.

Places for Civic Life

For decades, with a whole lot of mixed results, affordable housing was the province of the U.S. Department of Housing and Urban Development (HUD). Explaining his take on it, Baker says, "If HUD did a really great-looking project, people would say, 'You wasted taxpayer money.' From my point of view, Reagan basically killed HUD, and, strangely enough, Republicans came up with the idea of doing tax credits and privatizing the affordable housing business."

The move paved the way for nonprofits such as SAHA, which have shouldered the burden of defending the use of good design for people with the fewest economic resources.

"But assembling all the money is tricky," Friedland explains. "The Lakeside Senior Apartments would have been a perfect redevelopment project" before Governor Brown's cuts. "Instead, we had to piece it all together, and it's a thirty-million-dollar project."

Friedland estimates that there has been a drop from five new affordable housing projects each year to approximately one every other year following Brown's decision. "Even using all of the talent and resources and experience that we have as an organization," she continues, "it feels sometimes like just a drop in the bucket compared with the vast need in our communities."

Both Friedland and Baker remain optimistic about the future while acutely aware that housing of this type and quality remains limited. But that's not stopping seniors themselves from coming together to address their needs. There is a small but growing senior cohousing movement in the United States and an even stronger one internationally. There are also intentional communities across the country, including what are now referred to as NORCs, short for "naturally occurring retirement communities," where members more deliberately support one another in close proximity—down the block or just a few blocks away.

With housing projects of this type, Friedland's best advice for others in her position is to get the community engaged in a genuine way as early as possible: "If they're not on board, they will try to shut the project down in so many different ways. Then you're going to end up with huge compromises, and you may not even have a feasible project at all."

But she also believes that determining the right design and construction team is critical: "It's almost like we're artisanal developers. We don't bring that same team to every project. We look at each site uniquely. I think that's really important."

With its unique mix of public and private spaces and its proximity to Oakland's street life and lake, as well as its interior gathering spots, the Lakeside Senior Apartments in many ways embody the active streets that first sparked Friedland's interest in the built environment. The units themselves and their composition into a greater whole are the genius of Baker and his firm. It's the residents, such as Baugh, however, that make it feel like home.

Lakeside Senior Apartments

Location: Oakland, California, United States

Year completed: 2014

Built Area: 108,000 square feet

Cost (USD): $33.5 million

Client: Satellite Affordable Housing Associates
www.sahahomes.org

Design: David Baker Architects
www.dbarchitect.com

Photography: Bruce Damonte
www.brucedamonte.com
Brian Haux / Skyhawk Photography
www.skyhawkphoto.com

↑
**The main lobby area is
warmed by wood paneling
and lighting.**

6.
Raising Expectations
The Maternity Waiting Village in Malawi

→
Maternity Waiting Village in Kasungu, Malawi, by MASS Design Group, the University of North Carolina Project–Malawi, and the Malawi Ministry of Health; completed in 2015.

In January 2013, I improbably found myself seated before the president of a small country in East Africa. Before that trip, I probably couldn't even have placed Malawi on a map. Like many, I routinely expressed a love of Africa, and I had spent weeks at a time in various places on the continent, but Malawi was not among them.

Malawi is a staggeringly beautiful place, especially its countryside, where 85 percent of its population lives. It's also a country saddled with extreme poverty; most people survive as subsistence farmers on less than $2 per day.

As the guests assembled for the president, each of us was introduced—Former President of Ireland, Former President of Latvia, Former Vice President of South Africa, among others. When my turn came, I was introduced as the President of Public Interest Design, referring to the blog and website that I ran at the time, from my stately kitchen table in Brooklyn, New York. I looked around, and no one seemed to register the absurdity of it.

I was dwarfed by the powerful woman seated on an actual throne in front of me. President Joyce Banda was only the second female president in Africa, following in the footsteps of Liberian president Ellen Johnson Sirleaf. Elected vice president in Malawi's preceding election, Banda had ascended to the presidency in 2012 after the sudden death of her predecessor.

A top priority for Banda and her administration was maternal health. Malawi suffered from an extraordinarily high maternal mortality rate, where 1 in 36 mothers died during or immediately following childbirth. Only one country, Sierra Leone, had a higher maternal mortality rate at the time. For the sake of comparison, the rate is 1 in 2,400 in the United States.

As a mother, Banda took special interest in the problem. Even before becoming president, she was a member of the Global Leaders Council for Reproductive Health, coordinated by the Aspen Institute, the global think tank that had organized our visit. Banda called on the Aspen Institute's council to advise her new Presidential Initiative for Maternal Health and Safe Motherhood. The initiative was focused on reducing maternal mortality from its current rate to 115 or fewer per 100,000 live births.

A central component of Banda's initiative was getting more women to give birth in clinics that were staffed with health professionals and equipped to handle complications if they arose. Accordingly, she pledged to build as many as 150 "maternal waiting homes," which are effectively shelters or hostels near clinics, where women can stay for days or even weeks in advance of their due date. At the time of our visit, one of the new waiting homes was already in service and seven more were under construction across the country. Other countries, such as Zambia, were experimenting with similar shelters.

←
Women are interviewed in an informal maternal waiting home.

↙
Portrait of President Joyce Banda.

→
A government-designed maternal waiting home under construction.

Over several days, a small team and I visited informal maternal waiting homes, most being old buildings taken over by expectant mothers. On one rainy morning, we approached a small single-story cinder block building. Almost all its windows were broken or missing, with smoke soot around the outside of the window openings, indicating that fires had been used indoors for cooking or warmth.

That particular building was little more than a large open room, probably twenty by thirty feet in size. On the cold dirt floor were a couple dozen thin mats, and an assortment of rusty pans and dirty buckets were piled in one corner. Roughly two dozen women were sitting or standing around in the space, all dressed in colorful garments and headdresses.

Through a translator, I asked them what they thought of the makeshift shelter, and most of the mothers expressed gratitude for its mere existence. Virtually all said they missed their families and were often bored, with little to do. But they felt the effort outweighed the risk of being too far from a clinic at their time of birth. Some had walked for hours or even days to get there, and the prospect of doing so when in labor was much more daunting or impossible.

Outside, barely thirty feet away, stood the beginnings of one of the first maternal waiting homes built as part of Banda's initiative. Still under construction, it was a substantially larger building, several times the size and roughly twice the height of the informal shelter. Workers on scaffolding were finishing the exterior of its thick walls, which were clad in red bricks and a deep gray mortar.

The plans for these new structures were developed by Malawi's Ministry of Health. The structures took two forms: a twenty-four-bed version and a slightly larger thirty-six-bed structure. Each was projected to cost between $70,000 and $80,000 and would be funded by Malawi's private sector and outside philanthropic support.

The inside of the new structure was dark and damp, by-products of the rainy season but not helped by the design or construction. The walls were rough and the floors were little more than dirt. Several thick half-walls broke up the space but also blocked the little bit of light penetrating the relatively few small window openings. Moreover, there were no places to gather, to cook, or to learn new skills, be they crafts, farming, or otherwise.

Although I regret the comparison, to this day the only thing I can liken it to is a stable. This new building was unquestionably better than the co-opted building adjacent to it, but I believed that these women, particularly in this moment, deserved far better.

design for good

Raising Expectations

I'll never forget meeting those women and seeing those maternal waiting homes, both the informal ones in use and the new ones under construction. But I'll especially never forget sitting in Malawi's presidential palace and staring up at President Banda, flanked by her cabinet, staff, and other international aid leaders.

When it was my turn to brief the president, I cleared my throat, sat forward, and began to share my observations about what our team and I had seen in the preceding days. I spoke first about the extraordinary women and community health workers we had met. I projected on a screen several photographs of makeshift waiting homes and then several more of the larger government-built shelters under construction, including a close-up of a young male worker using a metal trowel to lay brick to the exterior. I sincerely commended the president and her staff for all of it, and she nodded approvingly.

I then mustered all the courage and respect that I could to tell the president that it wasn't enough and there might be a better way. I started by proposing simple program improvements, such as bathrooms, cooking areas, and places to gather. I talked about the dignity that these spaces could bring to the women's experience.

I then introduced a possible precedent in the Butaro Hospital in rural Rwanda, brought to life by MASS Design Group, Partners in Health, and that country's Ministry of Health, as detailed in chapter 1 of this book. As I showed one image after another of the Butaro Hospital, there were audible gasps in the room. From over a thousand miles away, they saw a new "possible." I explained that the hospital had also been built in a fraction of the time and for a fraction of the budget as Rwanda's other district hospitals and that it had employed local labor and local materials.

Numerous people—including aid leaders from the United Kingdom, Norway, and other countries—approached me after my remarks. Most significantly, I had a chance to meet with the architect from Malawi's Ministry of Health, who understood the value of places to gather, to cook, or to learn new skills. Within a day, he had updated the government plans to reflect each of them.

On one hand, it was startlingly easy to influence the Ministry of Health's design, which was set to be replicated across the country. On the other, I knew those small improvements still weren't enough. A bolder, more beautiful building was both needed and possible.

↑
A woman finds some solitude in one of the many small nooks throughout the Maternity Waiting Village.

→
Aerial view illustrating the building clusters and connected roofline.

I returned home to the United States determined to do something about what I saw as a huge need and opportunity. Katie Drasser, a close colleague at the Aspen Institute who had organized our delegation to Malawi, was equally determined.

Together, we were able to connect with an American doctor in the capital city of Malawi named Jeff Wilkinson. The University of North Carolina School of Medicine, where Wilkinson worked, had a special program on maternal health in Malawi. When we first met, Wilkinson and the university had just received a major grant from the Bill & Melinda Gates Foundation to catapult their maternal health work forward. It was Wilkinson's intention, as a small part of that work, to build two maternal waiting homes.

During our first phone call, I'm not sure that Wilkinson knew what to make of Drasser and me as we nervously pitched the opportunity for a more ambitious design for one or both of the two maternal waiting homes that he was embarking on. He was polite and seemingly intrigued but also clearly skeptical. As far as Wilkinson was concerned, he had viable plans for the two maternal waiting homes, issued by the government, no less. But, thankfully, he heard us out.

Design as a factor in health outcomes wasn't on Wilkinson's radar at that time. He tells me, "The hospital and the clinics and the operating room and the scalpel and the electrosurgery device were all things that were there to try to help improve a woman or a baby's life. But design wasn't at the forefront of my mind."

Raising Expectations

design for good

Raising Expectations

Still, I introduced Wilkinson to the work of MASS Design Group, hoping they might help convince him of the worthiness of not just constructing but truly designing a dignified place for these women.

Meanwhile, during one of my early conversations about the project with MASS, we talked about what I had seen in Malawi. I distinctly recall the organization's cofounder, Michael Murphy, advocating for private rooms for the women. Compared with the one-room informal waiting homes that I saw in use and the others under construction, it seemed like an extravagance even to me. For all my talk that everyone deserves good design, I still couldn't dream as big as Murphy.

Once they connected, Murphy and Wilkinson predictably hit it off. It was around that same time that I helped set up The Autodesk Foundation, and I was able to offer MASS a microgrant to underwrite its initial design work with Wilkinson. But thereafter, I effectively got out of the way, checking in with Murphy from time to time and little more.

This is where the story of a project like this would normally begin, with little understanding of how easily it might not have happened at all.

design for good

Murphy assigned one of MASS's directors, Patricia Gruits, to lead the project. Born near Detroit, Gruits went to design school at the University of Michigan, thereafter relocating to Boston. Before she joined MASS, Gruits had cofounded a nonprofit startup that provides a sustainable source of power and light in rural and low-income settings. Gruits quickly flew down from the MASS office in Kigali, Rwanda, where she was working on several other projects.

By that time, Wilkinson had selected a site in the Kasungu District, approximately two hours north of Malawi's capital city, Lilongwe, by car. From a review of the government plans and the information gathered to that point, Gruits presented a preliminary vision for a village that could foster a communal approach to improving health outcomes. "Just listening to her frame it in a language that a relative layperson could understand—in such a clear and concise way describing the impact of design on health and health-related behaviors—was like bells going off," Wilkinson recalls.

In considering this preliminary proposal that MASS presented, it was obvious to Wilkinson that if they were really going to design this village model together in a meaningful way, it wouldn't happen quickly. This was especially the case when a building like it hadn't been built in Malawi before. But even the predicted slowdown didn't deter Wilkinson's interest.

"It was very dramatic for me to believe the design of this project was worth doing, on top of my regular work of providing surgical services to women as I do, and also managing a multimillion-dollar grant," Wilkinson continues. "Patricia's argument and the way it was presented was convincing enough to say this is worth losing a significant amount of sleep and putting in a significant amount of additional effort."

With Wilkinson's support and to further inform their instinct about the village approach, Gruits and other MASS team members spent extensive time on-site. That initially meant interviewing and spending time with mothers, nurses, and other people who were on-site, which helped them ascertain specific needs and opportunities for the project. This immersive approach has long been a defining characteristic of MASS's work, dating back to the Butaro Hospital.

It's worth noting that there was already a tent on the Kasungu site, acting as a makeshift maternal waiting home. It provided Gruits with the opportunity to observe and interact with the mothers, albeit in a compromised environment. The makeshift nature of the tent meant that it had poor ventilation, which was compounded by the number of people who would crowd in when it was raining. Many people, Gruits learned and observed, ultimately opted to sleep in the rain outside under a tree, or next to a building, rather than in the tent.

When asked about what would improve their experience, the women Gruits interviewed talked about the need for basic services such as water. They all shared a single spigot for laundry, washing, and bathing. The water was supplied by an electric pump that was provided by the village, leaving the women's water source vulnerable to the country's routine power outages.

Gruits remembers asking the women what they missed about their homes. "I was expecting to hear something physical like a roof, my bed, my whatever. Instead, one of the women said, 'My children.' Another woman said, 'The ability to make money.' It caught me off guard in a lot of ways, but it also made me recognize the tensions that were on these women to be there and to receive safe health care."

The women were leaving their other children behind, along with opportunities to work, and a lot of them were primary breadwinners for their families. Gruits continues: "I think that's why we started to look at ways to create an empowering experience, so they might go home not just with a new baby but also with new skills or new ideas about things they could do."

MASS also worked with staff members of Malawi's Ministry of Health and Ministry of Transport and Public Works. In fact, Gruits and the team met with pretty much anyone who would talk to them. Echoing a key tenet of Banda's initiative, Gruits explains, "We knew the project wasn't just for the mothers; it's not just about creating these buildings, but working with communities to bring down the barriers for women to access care."

In the course of her interviews, Gruits was struck by a comment made by one of the nurses at the district hospital who was working with Wilkinson: "A waiting home should empower each woman, so that she goes back into her home a changed person, because that will encourage other mothers to go and wait there." Gruits adds, "If I have to put a finger on it, that is one of the ideas that really drove this project.

"Obviously, we wanted to make the project healthy, safe, and comfortable. But we really wanted to transform the idea of this being a waiting home into it being an empowering experience. We also wanted to build community among the mothers," Gruits explains. This sense of community, combined with the project's final form, ultimately came to influence its renaming as the Maternity Waiting Village.

MASS aspires to employ local labor and materials in every project it works on. But Gruits and her team worried that there wasn't an abundance of quality building materials local to Malawi. In such settings, brick made of local soil is often a solution. But in Malawi, the necessary firing of bricks is complicated by concerns about deforestation, since a great deal of wood is used in the process. Moreover, the bricks that were made locally really varied in terms of quality.

Malawi's unique climate was also a major driver in the selection of materials. Even access to native materials can change dramatically during the country's extreme rainy and dry seasons. Other materials, such as steel, wood, and even concrete, proved to be expensive or would have had to be imported.

Drawing on its experience in Rwanda, MASS decided to use compressed stabilized earth blocks, which are somewhat like bricks but don't require firing. The interlocking blocks are approximately twice the size of typical bricks and are made using an Auram Press, a manually operated machine that costs a few thousand dollars. That may not sound like much, but in the context of the budget, the expense seemed significant. Gruits and Wilkinson ultimately justified the cost, as the machine not only would ensure the use of local labor and materials for the project but also would become a community resource for use in future building projects.

The blocks quickly became central to the building's design, specifically its foundational piers, which are structural in nature, without reinforcement. Around the piers are three clusters of buildings, each containing twelve beds broken up into groups of four, achieving the Ministry of Health's thirty-six-bed goal. Within each cluster are two bathrooms, two showers, water storage, and a laundry room. There are additional kitchen and education spaces as well.

Beyond the piers, the walls themselves are also constructed of compressed earth blocks. During the day they absorb heat, which is then emitted at night. Generous roof overhangs provide shade in the dry season to ease heat gain within the walls, which then cool at night.

The walls and the structure's two roof configurations—one gabled and the other butterfly, so the inverse of gabled, almost like a saw pattern—work together, creating a seamless cover. This ensures shade during the hot, sunny months and shelter during the region's extensive rainy season.

"The design responds to many factors," explains Gruits. "It responds to the climate; it responds to the space limitations; it responds to creating a safe and healthy environment for mothers; and it responds to creating an empowering experience in some of the ancillary spaces outside the bedrooms themselves."

Back home in the United States, Gruits herself became a mother for the first time just as the Maternity Waiting Village was being completed in Malawi. "The American version of maternity, labor, and delivery is a very individualized experience. It's an experience we go through by ourselves or with our partner," she says. "I was in the hospital for three days and did not meet any other mothers or other babies being born. In Malawi, it's very different and much more of a community experience. Even just hanging out and waiting are completely different experiences in community," Gruits continues. "These women aren't sick; they're a healthy population just waiting together to go through what will hopefully be a very natural process."

Women gather at the Maternity Waiting Village.

Nurses and attendants smile with pride as a mother presents her newborn.

Gruits credits Wilkinson for green-lighting the project, and she never took his belief in her for granted. "Even though Jeff was tasked with this huge workload along with doing very important surgical work, he saw the value of design and of having a space that would dignify these women. Jeff's career is built on the premise that everyone deserves access to health care; I think he came to understand that a means to that is the belief that everyone deserves good design."

Gruits also praised Arthur Chiphiko, the Ministry of Health architect: "Arthur really opened himself up to an exchange of ideas. It wasn't just us, MASS, coming to Malawi and providing outside solutions to problems within their country; we were learning from Arthur and others."

The project was a learning experience for Wilkinson as well. "Working on the Maternity Waiting Village in Kasungu, I learned more about architecture and design and construction than I ever wanted to learn," he tells me with an appropriate mix of gratitude and exasperation.

The project in Kasungu was developed at the same time as a maternal waiting home in another part of Malawi called Area 25. The Area 25 home was built to the government's design specifications. "The two projects are literally day and night," Wilkinson explains. "The building in Area 25 is highly functional and perfectly adequate. In Kasungu, for a relatively similar price, we have something that transcends anything else that I've ever seen in this kind of environment.

"Aesthetically, there's simply no comparison," Wilkinson continues. "Even from the drawings and pictures that I had seen hundreds of times, I didn't really fully appreciate how aesthetically pleasing the Kasungu project was until it was completed and occupied. It really just flows so beautifully. It instantaneously gave me a sense of calm; there's something intrinsic about it that makes one feel that way.

"It made me wish that I had access to the same quality of consultation and involvement of personnel to make something like this happen in whatever construction project I'm about to undertake," says Wilkinson, now a professor at Baylor College of Medicine and continuing his work in Malawi. "The unfortunate reality is that it hasn't reached, in my naïve way of looking at it, a critical mass in order to become commonplace." Still, he's hopeful: "As people see that you can do this and it can be done in an affordable way and it has a positive impact, it will become much more commonplace."

When I asked Wilkinson who, aside from Gruits, most influenced his experience, he cited another MASS team member, Christian Benimana, a Rwandan architect who had spent time on-site in Malawi and had welcomed Chiphiko from Malawi's Ministry of Health and others to Rwanda to see MASS's work there.

"It's so clear to me that the level of quality and the level of attention to detail and Christian's expertise were really unparalleled. Christian is like Patricia's mirror image on this side of the world in terms of how they interact with people, their professionalism, their ability to explain complex ideas from a design and architectural standpoint to a novice," Wilkinson explains. "Those two, Patricia and Christian, make such a dynamic team."

Wilkinson encourages others in his position to connect with a design firm that, like MASS, has done work in resource-limited settings, so they don't stumble through some of the same problems. He is also a big believer in face-to-face meetings, despite also being a big believer in carbon offsetting.

"Every time we were together, we'd be driving along and Patricia would yell, 'Stop the car!' She'd run over to some brick and chip a piece off and pick up some dirt and taste it and wrap it up in tape and throw it against the wall, and then do a backflip over it," Wilkinson jokes. "She really lived the experience. I think having your partners come in and do that kind of stuff energizes you and makes you want to embrace the idea."

For Wilkinson, seeing is believing. "I think it's all about the partnership and exposure to a successful preexisting project. Anyone who's thinking about doing this needs to take a ride out to Kasungu, and then they'll just sign on the dotted line."

Wilkinson beautifully sums up the challenge and opportunity of building in these low-resource settings: "We're used to complex series of steps in medical procedures," he says. "And one intellectually understands the complexity of steps involved in other fields, but you simply can't fully appreciate them until you wade into them. Doing that in a low-resource setting and trying to bring the design into reality while having to minimize costs, while not compromising on quality, was probably the most challenging and surprising thing. It raised my awareness of what is possible."

Maternity Waiting Village

Location: Kasungu, Malawi

Year completed: 2015

Built Area: 6,500 square feet

Cost (USD): $196,000

Clients: University of North Carolina Project—Malawi www.med.unc.edu/infdis /malawi Malawi Ministry of Health

Design Entity: MASS Design Group, www.massdesigngroup.org

Photography: Iwan Baan www.iwan.com

↑
Elevation of the Maternity Waiting Village showing the sawtooth roof.

Raising Expectations

Conclusion
A Call to Expect More

Each project in this book holds lessons for those who want to dignify their lives and our shared world through design. Drawing on insights from my interview subjects and buildings they created together, I've identified five key lessons here.

→
Sharon Fieldhouse in Clifton Forge, Virginia, by design/buildLAB; completed in 2014.

↑
Hellen's House in Nakuru, Kenya, by Orkidstudio; completed in 2015.

design for good

Lesson 1: Embrace a Beginner's Mind-set

In our work lives especially, we are conditioned to think of or present ourselves as "experts." This assumes our studies, experiences, and skills establish a level of expertise worth imparting on others. But it risks our thinking that we have all the answers to a given problem without taking the time to fully understand the nuances of the situation, sometimes even blinding ourselves to the bigger picture. Embracing a "beginner's mind-set" is one way that all building contributors can not just humble ourselves but also gain entirely new knowledge and perspectives in the process.

A beginner's mind-set is a linchpin of the practice of human-centered design. One of the world's best-known firms, IDEO, and its nonprofit spinoff, IDEO.org, have emerged as two of the biggest advocates for human-centered design. IDEO.org cofounder Patrice Martin explains it this way: "What designers bring is the potential for new answers. While problems and needs may appear well-defined at the outset, we use a beginner's mind-set to take a step back and to breathe life and creativity into projects." Martin tells me, "It's about bringing in a fresh perspective and permission to look at the wider problem."

In their own ways, all building project stakeholders—clients, users, laborers, and others—have the potential to bring, and benefit from, a beginner's mind-set. The non-architects involved may very well be the best positioned to fuel innovation because of their perspectives. For me, that doesn't necessarily mean that those stakeholders will all belly up to tables with butcher paper and crayons to "codesign" projects, in the spirit of yesteryear's focus on "participatory design." Being human-centered doesn't mean denying that certain kinds of training prepare some people to drive the process and make important decisions at key moments. Instead, it means that all perspectives will be sought, heard, and honored throughout the design process.

The Butaro Hospital is the most storied example of a group of designers learning on the job. The group of Harvard graduate students inadvertently didn't make the same, often detrimental design decisions made in hospitals around the world, in part because they simply weren't experienced enough to be blinded by protocol. Their unorthodox decisions were driven by naïveté and necessity. They contended with issues such as limited electricity, an extremely tight budget, and the need to ensure natural airflow to safeguard against communicable diseases. Those limitations pushed them as designers and, ultimately, made the hospital more—not less—dignifying.

Other designers profiled here had never undertaken the particular project types they were presented with. Marina Tabassum's invitation to design a mosque in her home city, Dhaka, Bangladesh, is a prime example. Through research and her own intuition, Tabassum was able to forgo the symbols—domes, minarets, and the like—pervasive in so many other mosque designs. Her beginner's mind led to an elegance that simply would not have been possible had she been wedded to a "because we've always done it that way" mentality.

Lesson 2: Seek Partners, Not Clients

Architects and designers typically refer to the people they build for as "clients," which is why I use the term throughout the book. Unfortunately, the implications of that word are clear: the designer is the expert, hired by the client to provide a product or service that will—in theory—suit the needs of the client. It's top-down, and money is at the center of the relationship, neither of which bodes well for a dignifying process and outcome. It also puts a beginner's mind-set at risk.

The designers in this book are distinguished in seeing and treating the people they build with as partners, not clients. Money is obviously necessary to getting the work done, but it's not at the center of the relationship. And the relationship is reciprocal, not transactional, built on genuine respect for the insights that everyone brings.

When people feel like partners, not clients, they tend to want to work together over and over, as evidenced by repeat collaborations such as Skid Row Housing Trust's multiple projects with Michael Maltzan Architecture and, again, MASS Design Group's recurring work with both Partners in Health and Les Centres GHESKIO. It's also apparent in the way partners and designers talk about tackling difficult challenges together—solving problems, not pointing fingers.

Central Dallas Community Development Corporation and bcWORK-SHOP sat side by side in the same office over many of the years that they jointly worked on The Cottages at Hickory Crossing. It was a long haul, full of daunting bureaucratic and funding hurdles, but they stuck with it because they stuck together. With the added benefit of an unusually design-conscious funder, Kalamazoo College and Studio Gang pushed through several challenging features now central to the success of the Arcus Center for Social Justice Leadership, particularly its innovative exterior facade and its hearth and kitchen. The latter two

features required special approval and a shared commitment to seeing them through despite the odds.

It's important to acknowledge that individuals and entities undertaking design projects for the first time are putting just as much or more on the line as designers. To reap the full rewards of partnership, designers also have to take risks and push themselves. When both groups do, the payoff can be transformative.

Lesson 3: Build Community Support

I got goose bumps when the Atlanta BeltLine's founder, Ryan Gravel, described the community support that bubbled up in the early days of that project, "this truly, honest to God, grassroots movement of people who wanted something different. People fell in love with the vision for their future that was better than what they were seeing," he continued, "and better than what the city was offering them."

Traditionally, when it comes to built projects, the public has been seen as "stakeholders" at best and a hurdle at worst. Architects and their partners actually have an exciting opportunity to rally support for projects—to turn the public into a community. This isn't just about getting approval from a city council or planning department, important as that may be. It requires that designers, in particular, listen deeply to community needs, reflect those needs back to the stakeholders, and reinforce their understanding over time.

This goes beyond just "educating" the public, as it is often described; this is about imagining the potential impact together, building excitement around a project, and doing so collaboratively from an early stage. It is about seeing the public as the lifeblood of a future building, not an obstruction to be appeased. That kind of relationship building does wonders, not just for the reception of the original project but for its

long-term health. A community that "owns" a building or landscape project, that benefits from it in terms of their own quality of life, is one that takes care of it over time, no matter the economics.

Immersing designers in communities, especially ones they are not native to, is another meaningful way to gain crucial insights and build community support. When designers live among and with their partners, windows into the real, lived experiences of people, beyond the confines of an interview or focus group, open up. Relationships form around more than just the building objectives; they form around genuine discovery of living together, asking questions, learning about one another's quirks and qualities. That makes for a much stronger foundation for a building than any formal setting.

Lesson 4: Employ Workers and Source Materials Locally

In many respects, the work profiled in this book has set a new bar for designers when it comes to local labor and materials. Whether the two projects profiled herein by Rural Urban Framework in China, the Arcus Center's cordwood masonry, or the Butaro Hospital's intricate lava rock walls, the incredible contributions of local laborers and materials are tangible and stunning. Use of local resources matters because it minimizes projects' environmental impacts that come with transportation of materials and it maximizes positive impact on local economies.

You may have noticed the disproportionate number of projects built outside the United States that succeed most clearly on this front. When I mentioned the importance of local labor and materials in MASS's work in a keynote address for the American Institute of Architecture Students, a student afterward asked, "Why aren't U.S. projects held to that same standard?"

↖
Angdong Health Center in Baojing, Xiangxi, Hunan, China, by Rural Urban Framework and the Institute for Integrated Rural Development, Hong Kong; completed in 2012.

↑
John and Jill Ker Conway Residence in Washington, DC, by Sorg Architects, DLR Group, and Community Solutions; completed in 2016.

Talk about a great "beginner's mind" question. Indeed, why? Architects such as Michael Maltzan highlight very real challenges to that goal for projects within the United States. In Maltzan's case, the prefabricated construction method of the Star Apartments on Skid Row was already a stretch to get through city planning. Without viable options for those prefabricated units locally, Maltzan's firm had to go far outside the region, trucking materials in from out of state. After the project, Maltzan commendably set about working with the city to advocate for prefabrication, including local manufacturing facilities.

Brent Brown and bcWORKSHOP ultimately made a similar concession regarding the labor for The Cottages at Hickory Crossing, despite the extensive lead time on a nearly decade-long project. When construction finally got under way after ten hard-fought years, the organization abandoned its goal of employing future residents in the construction; it felt more compelled to get the units built quickly and get the residents into their homes. They'd waited so long already. It's understandable that the partners involved in this project sacrificed their original aspirations for local labor, and yet what was lost in the process?

But new projects afford the opportunity to find out. What lives might be transformed with new vocational skills and the inevitable boost in confidence that comes with being an integral part of a team that really and truly makes something? As this country and many others speculate about how to bring jobs back to underserved communities, recommitting to using local labor in all building projects is a small, but not insignificant, place to start.

Lesson 5: Measure Impact

Although "impact" has emerged as a buzzword in the social and philanthropic sectors, the influence of buildings on their communities can be difficult to measure. Projects can take years to realize—the Bait Ur Rouf Mosque in Dhaka took twelve years, and The Cottages at Hickory Crossing in Dallas took ten, as just two examples. Designers also traditionally have very limited interaction with a project once a building is occupied. So how can we measure the impact of a building, and by what standards?

Those interested in the social and economic impact of buildings have a viable precedent in the U.S. Green Building Council's Leadership in Energy and Environmental Design (LEED) program. LEED certifies buildings and even entire neighborhoods on the basis of an array of factors including energy efficiency, water usage, and proximity to transit, among many others. It also accredits individual professionals— from a wide range of disciplines, not just design.

Since the LEED rating system's launch in 2000, nearly 80,000 projects—representing more than 15 billion square feet of commercial and institutional space as well as 250,000 residential units—have been certified as part of the program. These projects are located in all fifty U.S. states and in 161 countries and territories. Without national or international standards such as LEED's, design firms, organizations, and their partners in building projects are left to their own devices to determine what to measure regarding social and economic impact and how to do so.

Some organizations, for a variety of reasons, including their dependence on philanthropic funding, are investing heavily in assessing their impact. MASS Design Group, once again, maintains a robust spreadsheet accounting for overall costs as well as breakdowns for labor, materials, and transportation, among many other indicators. The organization tracks those costs that fall within the immediate local community (MASS considers anything within a radius of 100 kilometers, about 62 miles, to be local and anything within 800 kilometers, about 497 miles, to be regional). In addition to carefully tracking the number of people employed in the construction of its buildings, MASS works with its partners to track the primary and secondary users of their spaces, year over year.

Entities such as Central Dallas Community Development Corporation, Satellite Affordable Housing Associates, and Skid Row Housing Trust all track impact by their own metrics. As multi-time clients, each has the added benefit of being able to track data across similar projects, providing points of comparison. In many respects, the Atlanta BeltLine has the ability to do the same, across many neighborhoods and conditions, to see how its trails and parks function.

It's time for rigorous assessment of impact to become standard for all buildings, with funds allocated to do so. One existing, if little used, tool is the post-occupancy evaluation—a rigorous study that asks users about their actual experiences of buildings paired with observation of users' behaviors, most often conducted by third parties. Such data can ensure that the best or most successful aspects of buildings are understood and challenges are remedied or not repeated in future projects. Post-occupancy evaluations are occasionally administered by government agencies, such as the Department of Housing and Urban Development or the General Services Administration in the United States, but are rarely included in a project scope.

Just as the nonprofit sector has become vigilant about utilizing independent researchers to evaluate the impact of their work—frequently in the form of "randomized control trials," popularly known as RCTs—it's time for those of us who build to get curious about how our creations stand up in the long run.

→
Swawou Layout Community Primary School for Girls in Kenema, Sierra Leone, by Orkidstudio and the Swawou School Foundation; completed in 2016.

design for good

As I was writing this book, listening to people from around the world and all walks of life talk about design, I started to connect the dots on various systemic shifts that will have to take place if more of this work is to be realized in the coming years. What follows are five of the foremost needs, which I encourage appropriate institutions to see as opportunities. Some are not new, but the need for them is greater than ever.

Need 1: Dramatically Evolve Design Education and Training

Decades after the founding of community engagement programs like the celebrated Rural Studio design/build program at Auburn University, such opportunities for architecture and design students remain outliers. Many are literally seen as extracurricular. It is admittedly difficult to squeeze these opportunities into tightly packed semesters and academic calendars, but it's time we insist on doing so. Save for some unique unaccredited programs, such as the nonprofit Archeworks in Chicago, design schools in the United States have yet to put a stake in the ground and use their resources in a way that clearly prioritizes the public good across an entire curriculum.

Numerous practitioners in this book, be they MASS cofounders Michael Murphy and Alan Ricks or Orkidstudio founder James Mitchell, talked about embarking on this type of work not because of but in spite of their education. All three of these designers remain actively involved with the academy and grateful for their training in critical thinking, but they wish students had greater opportunities to directly apply their learning.

While Western architecture students need more opportunities to learn about and actually participate in this kind of work, it's even more important that the pool of non-Western architects be expanded and elevated. There are currently approximately 40,000 architects on the entire African continent—a jaw-dropping number when you consider how much building will go on in the increasingly urbanizing continent in the next decade. By comparison, the United States has roughly 100,000, or two and one-half times as many, while the country is a fraction the size of Africa.

Recognizing this, MASS helped to establish Rwanda's first architecture program within the Kigali Institute of Science and Technology. The organization has employed multiple graduates of the program. More recently, MASS launched the first-of-its-kind African Design Centre, led by Rwandan architect Christian Benimana. In its inaugural year, the African Design Centre welcomed eleven fellows from seven African countries, along with one fellow from Brazil. The fellows gain an array of hands-on skills training and construction experience.

Benimana explains: "Eventually, I hope the African Design Centre will be a hub for the most creative minds, where the world turns for solutions—not just for the continent but for all these big global challenges that we're faced with. The way we build will be as important as what we build."

→
**Butaro Doctors'
Sharehousing in Burera,
Rwanda, by MASS Design
Group and Brigham and
Women's Hospital;
completed in 2015.**

Need 2: Increase Demand for Design

Despite all the goodwill and ambition on the part of designers, the social sector's demand for design remains comparatively low. There is a missing link between an overwhelming supply of design and people knowing how to tap into it.

Pro bono design projects—whereby firms reduce or waive their fees—for many years represented my highest aspiration for scaling up design to reach those who normally don't benefit from it. A decade ago, colleagues and I launched a pro bono program that asked architecture and design firms across the United States to dedicate 1 percent of their billable hours—just twenty hours per employee per year—to organizations that could not otherwise afford them.

Modeling our efforts on the legal profession's pro bono law movement, we tapped into a desire on the part of many design professionals to give back. At their best, these efforts leveraged the resources of entire firms—yielding new models of housing for nonprofits such as Habitat for Humanity or community centers, schools, and other buildings. We witnessed a surge in pledges, with upward of 1,500 firms signing on over the course of the next decade. Oddly, nonprofits—which far outnumber for-profit firms in the United States, by a factor of at least 15 to 1—never flooded the program.

Why? Most people, especially nonprofit leaders focused on underserved populations, probably assume that architects simply work with rich people or corporations—end of story. Many don't know what design is in the first place, and those who have some inkling often don't make the connection to their own work. They have no idea, in other words, how critical design could or should be to their existing mission.

If any one organization is shifting the average person's relationship to design at a significant scale, it is IDEO.org. The organization has invested significant resources in codifying its human-centered design approach, producing guidebooks, case studies, and a wildly popular online course, which is uniquely paired with on-the-ground teamwork and experiences. When IDEO.org launched its online program in 2013, it had 13,000 registrants from around the world. Just three years later, in 2016, it had a staggering 62,000 from over one hundred countries.

"When we show up now to work with organizations that we're partnering with, they've already done the course. Their rooms are covered in sticky notes; they're primed and ready," says IDEO.org cofounder Patrice Martin. "You don't actually have to be a sophisticated 'capital D Designer' who knows how to make everything beautiful, considered, intentional, and joyful—which I fundamentally am a huge proponent of—to participate in how you bring desirability into all the systems and services that the world relies on."

Just as the Butaro Hospital has become a well-known success story, we need many more in other sectors. The projects on these pages would be a good place to start. Imagine not just a hospital but an entire health-care system in the United States that is designed to dignify, such as the stunning example of Kaiser Permanente, which my family and I happily rely on for health care in California. Or not just a single well-designed charter school but entire school districts. From a civic standpoint, the High Line, the park that repurposed an abandoned elevated railway on the West Side of Manhattan, is another possible precedent, but we need many more.

Clients and users need the chance to speak much more publicly on behalf of these projects, which is why their voices figure so prominently in this book. These groups need to be empowered as ambassadors for design, and designers as advocates for their causes, be it education, health, housing, or otherwise.

Need 3: Form Alliances and Unite Disparate Groups around Shared Values

Just as the projects in this book demonstrate the value of partnerships, the larger field of design would benefit greatly from a far deeper bench of allies. Each and every one of the challenges facing our world is complex and requires a systemic approach. So it's time the design field and design standards better reflect what fields such as public health, as but one example, know about the built environment.

Movement scholars such as University of Virginia professor Barbara Wilson have been vocal advocates for design to align more closely with the fields of public health, global development, and others. Wilson can point to multiple movements over the course of history that have grown and succeeded thanks to powerful and long-lasting alliances.

Wilson specifically identifies the disability rights movement, which united seemingly disparate populations ranging from the blind and deaf communities to veterans injured in the line of duty. "Instead of fracturing around disagreements and differences," Wilson explains, "these groups worked to keep the frame as wide as possible. They ended up thinking about disability not as a personal medical limitation but instead as a shared environmental limitation.

"That language took decades to develop," Wilson continues, "but it's incredibly powerful because every single person in the entire world should care about disability rights. We're all going to get sick or grow old at some point in our life, or care for someone who is."

These types of alliances need to be strategically sought out, cultivated, and based on mutual respect and trust. It's unfortunately not simply putting field leaders in a room for a day or two, as a sort of meeting of the minds, but instead doing the slow work of building actual relationships. While the investment is significant, the payoff is well worth it.

Need 4: Increase Funding for This Work

The past decade has seen steady growth in philanthropic funding for design. There are now program officers in most major foundations who see design as part of their tool kit. Many smaller foundations have the same. On several occasions, the National Endowment for the Arts and other entities have even gathered design funders together to build community and comradery.

Despite all this progress, however, design remains on the far periphery of the philanthropic sector, compared with issues such as education, the environment, and health. Rather than advocating that design, in and of itself, should rise to the same level of consideration as these issues, I believe designers and foundations themselves would be better served to talk about design as a largely untapped resource to uniquely address issues such as education, the environment, and health.

Although human-centered design, in particular, has captured the imagi-nation and attention of foundations, most remain averse to specifically supporting design and building projects in particular. This strikes me as ironic when one considers the offices and buildings that most of these foundations occupy. Most are substantially nicer than the offices occu-pied by their grantees. Foundations clearly understand the power of good design as it relates to their own quality of life and state of being. Why wouldn't they want the same for the people whom they serve?

There are clearly funders and even foundations that put their money where their mouth is when it comes to design. Philanthropist Jon Stryker of the Arcus Foundation has done so multiple times, including with the Arcus Center for Social Justice Leadership in Kalamazoo,

Michigan. Other individual donors, such as Ho Shu Leong, who sponsored Mulan Primary School in China, play critical roles. Indeed, the Clinton Foundation played an essential role in the lead-up to the Butaro Hospital in Rwanda. The Bill & Melinda Gates Foundation funded the Maternity Waiting Village in Malawi. But a clearer commitment on the part of the philanthropic sector at large is both needed and warranted.

Need 5: Be Proactive; Be of Service

This final need is directed—even more than the others—to my fellow designers. It's time we designers stop waiting for opportunities to come to us. Instead, as evidenced in these pages, designers have the chance to seek out projects and to partner with entities that have never before benefited from design. This needs to be done at a scale and a pace that we've not attempted before. Because that's what the world needs.

Too many designers continue to wait for the phone to ring or to be asked to take on a project. Countless others pour themselves into conceptual design competitions, while those designs have little chance of seeing the light of day, much less improving people's lives. It's time that designers stop this harmful practice of throwing their time and ideas and money away through competitions, and instead invest those resources into design that could make a difference in the world. This book is filled with examples of designers and projects that have done just that, with critical insights about building trust with historically overlooked communities and populations. Indeed, not a single project in this book was born of a design competition.

Circling back to where we began, with the work that MASS Design Group initiated with Partners in Health, it seems apt to consider Dr. Paul Farmer's lens of a "preferential option for the poor." The idea—adopted from liberation theology—is that the poor deserve the best-quality intervention because they've been given the least by luck and circumstance. This applies to design just as much as it applies to Farmer's field of global health.

What inspired me to write this book operates on two levels. On one level, as this conclusion suggests, my motivation is deeply pragmatic: I want to change the practice of architecture and design. I want to alter how we build, what we build with, and who we build for. On another level, I'm a believer in the power of design to change lives and to bring dignity to average people, the disenfranchised, and the poor.

I don't shy away from my role as an evangelist, out in the world, trying to convince people of the ethical imperative of bringing good design to all people. In a time of such heightened inequality, the ethical dimension of this has never felt more important.

I am reminded of the words of British philosopher Alain de Botton in his book *The Architecture of Happiness*: "Belief in the significance of architecture is premised on the notion that we are, for better and for worse, different people in different places—and on the conviction that it is architecture's task to render vivid to us who we might ideally be."

Well-designed spaces are not just a matter of taste or a question of aesthetics; they literally shape our ideas about who we are and what we deserve in the world.

That is the essence of dignity.

And both the opportunity and the responsibility of design.

For good.

And for all.

Acknowledgments

Design for Good would never have happened without the unrelenting support of my partner in life and in work, journalist Courtney Martin. She helped me conceive of almost every aspect of the book, and she meticulously edited the text at multiple turns. Our older daughter, Maya, is known to tell people, "Momma is a writer, and Dada is an exerciser," so I hope this book may position me for a promotion in her big blue eyes.

I am extremely grateful to Melinda Gates for her eloquence in writing the foreword to this book. The design field is incredibly fortunate to have such an invaluable champion. My sincere thanks also go to Clare Doody, Ellie Schaack, and the one and only Catherine St. Laurent.

The two years that I invested in researching projects, interviewing people, and writing *Design for Good* was made possible through the support of multiple individuals and entities. I'd like to especially thank Cliff Curry and Delight Stone, founders of the groundbreaking Curry Stone Design Prize, as well as Kyle Reis and The Reis Foundation, for their generosity.

This book is also made possible through a major grant from the National Endowment for the Arts. I want to acknowledge Jason Schupbach, the NEA's past director of design and creative placemaking programs, as a foremost champion of design within both the federal government and the philanthropic sector for seven prosperous years.

Numerous design industry leaders have helped get this book out into the world. Among many others, they include Jennifer Busch, Laura Marlow, Oriana Reich, John Rouse, John Stephens, and Jon Strassner. I am grateful for their role in dramatically expanding the reach of this book.

My immense thanks to Heather Boyer, Maureen Gately, Meredith Harkel, Julie Marshall, Rachel Miller, Sharis Simonian, and their colleagues at Island Press for publishing this book, as well as Maura Harris for her eagle-eye copyediting. I remain deeply drawn to the mission of Island Press, itself a nonprofit organization, and encourage its support.

The astonishingly wise David Dewane and my longtime collaborator Katie Crepeau both provided crucial editing and research assistance. I want to also thank Judy Wert for her management wisdom and Caroline Horswill for her administrative support. Sincere thanks to my FRESH Speakers partner Vanessa Valenti for her support as the book was in development.

It was a dream come true, once again, to work with designers Paula Scher and Courtney Gooch and their talented team at Pentagram, including project manager Dehlia Hennessy Brown. Simply put, they are the best of the best.

A disproportionate number of images in the book were captured by Iwan Baan, one of the most innovative architectural photographers of our time. My thanks to Iwan for his friendship and generosity and also to his assistant, Suzanne Tóth-Pál, for our countless exchanges.

All told, I conducted over one hundred interviews for this book with people in dozens of countries and almost every time zone. I am humbled by each and every person who took the time to share their stories and ideas with me. In addition to those cited in the text, the book benefited greatly from the examples and insights of Andrew Balster, Thatcher Bean, Phil Bernstein, Mia Birdsong, Jamie Blosser, David Bornstein, Angela Brooks, Eric Cesal, Krista Donaldson, Theodore Eccleston, Peter Eliassen, Sunny Fischer, Natalie Foster, Jess Garz, Aaron Hurst, Theresa Hwang, Megan Jett, Aaron Koch, Emi Kolawole, Brad Leibin, Jonathan Lundstrom, Wendy MacNaughton, Ashley Marsh, Jody McGuire, Gilad Meron, John Ochsendorf, Liz Ogbu, Jennifer Pahlka, Raul Pantaleo, Caroline Paul, Casius Pealer, Emily Pilloton, Amy Ress, Ellen Rudolph, Tia Salmela Keobounpheng, Mia Scharphie, Jacques Sebisaho, Marika Shioiri-Clark, Chuck Slaughter, Cynthia Smith, Suman Sorg, Mary Speaker, Joe Speicher, Kevin Starr, Katie Swenson, Naomi Swinton, Graham Veysey, and Jocelyn Wyatt, Keith Zawistowski, and Marie Zawistowski. My confidence in the future of design and the social sector rests in these visionary leaders.

I am fortunate to have many extraordinary colleagues at TED, my principal client, who have taught me the power of ideas. I would like to thank my close collaborators Chris Anderson, Juliet Blake, Patrick D'Arcy, Hasiba Haq, Emily McManus, Pat Mitchell, Dan Pallotta, Chee Pearlman, Tom Reilly, Ella Saunders-Crivello, Kelly Stoetzel, Danielle Thomson, Helen Walters, and especially the guiding light of Anna Verghese. In one of the most powerful TED talks I've ever seen, Dr. Suzanne Barakat challenged viewers to put their professional skills to work in combating Islamophobia; her talk inspired me to seek out a mosque project for this book. The Bait Ur Rouf Mosque quickly became one of my favorite projects.

Special thanks go to my colleagues at the Aspen Institute, including Katie Drasser and Peggy Clark, who organized our fateful trip to Malawi in January 2012, and also to Andrew Quinn and Rachael Strecher with the institute's New Voices Fellowship program for emerging leaders in global health and development.

Much of the early conceptual research for this book was supported by my mentor Thomas Fisher during his long tenure as dean of the College of Design at the University of Minnesota and by our close colleague Trevor Miller. I also want to acknowledge Jennifer Wolch, dean of the College of Environmental Design at the University of California, Berkeley, and Geraldine Forbes Isais, dean of the School of Architecture and Planning at the University of New Mexico, for inviting me to give commencement addresses on the topic of dignity. During this same period, the *New York Times* published an essay that I coauthored with my wife, Courtney, titled "Dignifying Design," which directly inspired this book.

Many other experiences informed it, however. Chief among them was curating the *Public Interest Design: Products, Places & Processes* exhibition with Jason Medal-Katz, Matt Tierney, and Roddy Wykes at the Autodesk Gallery in San Francisco. More recently, I have found an invaluable community and creative outlet in photography, fueling both my sense of beauty and my writing. I want to especially thank Adam Ali, Larry Billimek, Engel Ching, Jason Fernschuss, Michael Hindman, Vincent James, Jeff Lewis, Long Luc, Illy Manor, Tracie Tanakaya, Mahesh Thapa, and Stephen Wilkes, from whom I learn so much.

My parents, Mary and John Cary, a retired nurse and a more-than-thirty-five-year nonprofit director, respectively, raised me to care for other people with my whole heart. Even from a distance, my big Irish Roman Catholic family, complete with five siblings and a gaggle of spouses, nieces, and nephews, is a huge part of my life, enthusiastically supporting my work. If any two people read every word of this book, it will be my eighty-some-year-old grandmother Audrey Gorwitz in Oshkosh, Wisconsin, and my uncle Tom Cary, who lives in veterans' housing in Milwaukee. Thanks as well to my wonderful in-laws, Jere and Ron Martin, for their continuous love and support.

More than anyone or anything, however, Courtney, Maya, and Stella are the center of my universe; they teach me daily about the power of design as I watch them experience the world. We are truly blessed to live in the beautiful San Francisco Bay Area in a unique cohousing community called Temescal Commons. The twenty-five members with whom we share our lives are like family to us. Our physical spaces were designed with utmost grace and intention; it is the first truly dignifying place that I've ever lived in. Words cannot express how grateful I am to the founders and architects of Temescal Commons for giving my family and me such a special place to call home.

About the Author

An architect by training, John Cary has devoted his career to expanding the practice of design for the public good. John's first book was *The Power of Pro Bono: 40 Stories about Design for the Public Good by Architects and Their Clients*. His writing on design, philanthropy, and fatherhood has appeared in the *New York Times*, on CNN.com, and in numerous other publications.

John works as a philanthropic advisor to an array of foundations and nonprofits around the world, and he frequently curates and hosts events for TED, the Aspen Institute, and other entities. Deeply committed to diversifying the public stage, he is a founding partner in FRESH Speakers, a next-generation speakers bureau that represents young women and people of color. For seven years, John served as executive director of the nonprofit Public Architecture, building the largest pro bono design program in the world, pledging tens of millions of dollars in donated services annually.

A native of Milwaukee, Wisconsin, John is a graduate of the University of Minnesota and the University of California, Berkeley. He is a fellow of the American Academy in Rome, a resident of the Rockefeller Foundation's Bellagio Center, and a three-time commencement speaker, among other honors.

John lives in Oakland, California, with his wife, author Courtney E. Martin, and their two daughters, Maya and Stella.

Appendix

Photography
Credits